Setup Reduction for Printers

A Practical Guide to Reducing Makeready Time in Print Manufacturing

Authored by:

Malcolm G. Keif

Kevin Cooper

Setup Reduction for Printers

A Practical Guide to Reducing Makeready Time in Print Manufacturing

Malcolm G. Keif
Kevin Cooper

Additional copies may be ordered at http://www.keif.com/SetupReduction
For correspondance or bulk purchases, please contact: SetupReduction@keif.com

Book Design: Trevor Schroeder
Cover Design: Trevor Schroeder, Malcolm G. Keif, Donna Templeton

Printed in the United States of America

Library of Congress Control Number: 2011914597

ISBN-13: 978-0615524733
ISBN-10: 0615524737

10 9 8 7 6 5 4 3 2 1

Table of Contents

Acknowledgement

We would like to thank the many people who have influenced and helped us develop the concepts presented in this book. Many have gone before us and laid the foundation of setup reduction, especially Mr. Shingo and others in various fields of manufacturing. In the printing industry, we acknowledge those who have provided advice; others have allowed us to work with them in helping their organizations reduce setup times. All have been instrumental in helping us progress as Lean thinkers.

Thanks goes to many industry leaders but particularly Lloyd Streit and Jeff Salisbury for their trust in us. We also acknowledge those who have attended our workshops and seminars over the years and shared constructive feedback and stories.

Special thanks goes to Trevor Schroeder, Donna Templeton, and Steve Schulte for their help with layout, design, illustrations, and concepts.

Our colleagues are great! Thanks to those we work with in the Graphic Communication Department at Cal Poly, as well as the many support organizations across campus. There is no better staff than the faculty, office folks, and technicians in our department.

And most importantly, thanks goes to the Keif family and the Cooper family for their tireless support of us; and the efforts necessary to publish a book of this type. We so appreciate their support.

1 Value Creation: The Reason for Setup Reduction

This book is about makereadies—those critical tasks involved in setting up a printing press, rewinder, converting machine or binder. It is about the time spent changing from one job to another and how to minimize that time. While it is far too ambitious to give you step by step procedures for setting up every piece of equipment in the printing industry, this book will help you by outlining principles for reducing your makeready time... a lot!

It may be obvious, but makereadies are not something customers value. Why should you care? After all, customers know that makereadies are part of printing and they simply have to pay for them. It is part of the process. Printers, converters, and bookbinders build makeready time into their pricing and customers know that it is a cost of doing business. So, why is it important to reduce makeready time? If I estimate an hour makeready, the customer pays for an hour of makeready, and my pressroom uses an hour of makeready, who cares?

One of the foundational premises of this book is that the creation of *customer value* is paramount—it is the core focus of your business. *Value creation*, as defined by the customer, is the central goal for all printers and converters. This simple concept is what separates the best companies from average companies. It is why the best printers spend significant energy and resources trying to find out what their customers want and continually search for solutions for their customers' problems. It forms the basis for equipment purchases and new technique or application launches.

> Value creation is the goal of every business. It is the process of producing activities, products or services that are desired by customers. In contrast, non-valued items are those that a customer may reluctantly purchase because it is "part of the process." Leaders focus on increasing valued activities and reducing non-valued activities (waste). Makeready is nearly always considered a non-valued activity

What customers' find to be of value is not always easy to define. If I knew precisely what really delighted my customer, I could focus exclusively on that and have a customer for life. I would have customers who will gladly pay reasonable prices, and perhaps even premium pricing, because they are delighted with my products and services. Again, this seems pretty obvious. Maybe your business already enjoys this scenario but many do not. Most try to figure out how to be different from their competitors but do not really know what their customers want, other than cheap prices and faster turn-around times.

One way to visualize value creation is to imagine everything itemized on an invoice—Everything! Sales representatives' time (or commission), the estimate, customer service or project management, all consumables, makeready costs, actual printing and bindery costs, and even a portion of general and administrative (G&A) overhead. Which items do you think your customers would call about and question? Probably things like sales costs, estimating costs, customer service costs, makeready costs, and G&A overhead. These items are generally not highly valued by your customer. Are they necessary? In most cases, yes. But that does not mean they are valued. Which items on that same invoice would your customer deem reasonable? Those are the valued items. If you want to be a high-profit printer, you figure out ways to reduce the time used for non-valued processes and determine ways to increase the time used for valued processes.

Invoice—Please pay this amount

Estimating	$75.00
Project Management	$120.00
File Management/Prep	$45.50
Plates	$50.00
Makeready	$175.00
Printing/Converting	$3815.00
Total	$4280.50

So, recognizing that processes that are not valued exist, we are in the habit of burying those costs in an invoice. And that may well be the best way to hide from the customer those items they don't "value". But the best companies— those who understand the concept of value—look to reduce those tasks and put increased focus and attention on providing services that customers are delighted about paying for. Will non-valued processes ever go away? Some items may but likely not all. Will makereadies ever go way? Probably not entirely. But that does not mean we do not put focused attention on the items customers do not value and work to reduce them. Makeready reduction is important. It is not an option. It is a necessity to increase customer loyalty and to remain competitive. Even if you have customers who do not object to paying for setup costs, you certainly improve your competitive position by being able to reduce, or minimize, setup time and expense. You create a durable competitive advantage over your rivals. So, now that that is out of the way, let us start to focus on Setup Reduction.

Productivity: How Much Value is Created During a Production Shift?

Just how much press-time does the average printer actually use to print sellable product? That is an interesting question and one that many printers cannot answer precisely. Of course, if you do very long runs you may spend the majority of a shift printing with little downtime. On a good shift you may never stop the press or binder unless you have to do a brief cleaning activity (like washing blankets). If that is the case, you may conclude that you produce sellable work for 11.5 hours out of a 12-hour shift. That level of productivity is great...at least for that shift.

If you have shorter run lengths (and I bet you do), you may only produce sellable work 50% or less of the time in a shift. But whether you do long runs or short runs is not the point. The point is:

- Do you know how productive you are and are you focused on becoming more productive?

And equally important:

- Do you define productivity in terms of value creation?

Some printers do track productivity but most collect no data that really tells them how much value is being created during a shift. Further, most printers include makeready in their productivity numbers, noting that it is chargeable. So is productivity the same as value creation? Not when you include non-value items in your productivity equation. *Printing Industries of America* (PIA), *Tag and Label Manufacturers Institute* (TLMI), and other trade associations track industry productivity ratios. PIA offers great resources for benchmarking sheetfed offset press operations. Some of their publications break out different activities of a press run including makeready. Check them out if you would like to see where you fit compared with the average. But let me caution you, you cannot settle for being average, or even above average. You can only settle on maximizing value creation for your customers. Anything less is a problem and must result in a conscious effort for improvement.

Let us start by breaking down all the things that happen during a typical press or bindery shift (you can certainly add or take away from this list to personalize it for your company):

Shift changes:	many press teams have a structured or informal meeting during a shift change.
Read job ticket:	understand the materials and job parameters.
Stage materials:	acquire the appropriate ink, stock, signatures, etc.
Locate tooling:	locate the appropriate tools, equipment, supplies, and parts for the job.
Makeready:	setting up the press, rewinder, folder, cutter, or binder, achieving registration, color, and maximum throughput.
Production:	making sellable product (i.e. printing, die cutting, stitching)
Cleaning:	cleaning in and around the work area.

Maintenance:	fixing both minor and major equipment failures and/or preventing problems.
Breaks:	work breaks for human function and required by law.
Meetings:	department meetings for training or setting policy.
Visiting, talking:	socialization of the work crew.

When you look at this list you may think, "Sure, a few of those things are bad but most are just part of printing." True enough. But one of the first shifts you must make in your thinking is that when you are focusing on value creation, you are not judging the merits or necessity of activities. It is not a situation of value-creation being good and everything else is evil. It is a situation of understanding and emphasizing what customers want. Customers want magazines, bags, books, cartons, labels, flyers, or whatever the printed product is. In truth, they want increased sales, branding, marketing, point-of-sale purchases, and compelling packaging. Print is a great tool to achieve those things. But everything that does not directly influence creation of valued products and services should be reduced to the smallest amount of time possible.

So, let us get back to the question at hand. How productive are you? Productivity can be defined as the ratio of chargeable time to staffed time. Most printers include makeready in with the run when calculating productivity (the rationale is that makeready is chargeable). And most commercial and publication printers are in the 70-85% range of productivity. Packaging printers are often lower, in the 60-75% range, due to increased customization and complexity. Of course that varies a lot by company. A company who is 75% productive means that 25% of the time in a 12-hour shift (3 hours) is not used for makeready or run. Those hours are spent reading job tickets, staging materials, locating tools, cleaning, maintaining equipment, taking breaks, visiting the "lunch wagon", or just chatting with other employees.

Now how much of that 75% is in value creating activities (producing valued products and services)? The number goes down further, likely closer to 50% or less for many companies. Quite possibly, only half of the time you are staffing your equipment is used for creating valued products for customers.

What should you expect? We are dealing with humans here, right? Can you really expect them to be 100% productive? Not likely, but there is plenty of room for improvement. As important as having a value creation benchmark is understanding the *reason* why focusing on value creation is so important. It will drive everything you do in the pressroom or bindery.

When you undertake a press, converting, or finishing activity…any activity… ask yourself the question: "Does this create value (remember, value is defined by your customer—it is not value just because you make something or do something)?" If that answer is yes, try to do more of it. If the answer is no, try to do less of it. That singleness of mindset will help you become more competitive. World-class printers think this way, both in management and on the production floor.

The Benefits of Setup Reduction

Reducing makeready time provides substantial benefits. A shorter makeready means lower costs that can be passed along, in part or entirety, to the customer. If you can reduce average makeready time from one hour to 45 minutes, those 15 minutes are compounded many times over in a week, saving thousands of minutes and ultimately dollars. Lower costs certainly offer a competitive pricing advantage and also a means to increase profit margins.

A less obvious benefit of reducing makeready time is an increase in available press or bindery hours to sell. While this may sound insignificant, where else can you gain equipment capacity with no additional investment? If you can save four hours of makeready time over a two-week window, you can sell four more hours of press or bindery time. That is significant!

You also have the potential to lower your hourly equipment rates depending on how they are calculated. If you already include every second of makeready time as billable and part of your productivity formula, you may not actually have a decrease in hourly rates. But the effect is the same: you can sell more jobs over that same window of time. So, whether your rate decreases or your billable hours increase, the end result is more income per unit of time.

Reducing makeready time can also play a significant continuous improvement role. Setup Reduction brings problems to the surface more quickly. Many of the principles around Setup Reduction were developed by the Toyota Motor Corporation during the 1950's and 1960's. Toyota received some bad publicity in recent years. This was primarily

Benefits of Setup Reduction
Lower costs
More structure/ attention to detail
Increased capacity
Errors discovered more quickly (i.e. plates)
Discover inefficient processes more quickly
More customer value

due to their momentarily straying from the very principles that built their success. They made mistakes. But they are still one of the leading automobile producers and a model for manufacturing excellence.

One of key principle of Toyota is to try to expose fundamental problems so they can be addressed, rather than allow them to remain hidden. Reducing makeready will help to expose weaknesses in your production system. You may ask yourself, "Why in the world would I want to do that?" In the short-term you may find it painful to expose problems but for long-term improvement, you must find out your shortcomings and address them. They are there whether you choose to find and acknowledge them or not. The best printing and packaging companies are not afraid to find their weak points. In fact, they thrive on discovering shortcomings in their workflow, operations or administrative practices. Reducing makeready time will help you see where you are weak with staging materials, reducing work in process inventory, teamwork, and other processes.

Have you noticed that customers want shorter run lengths? Setup Reduction allows your customer to reduce inventory and make short-notice changes to product literature, SKUs, or whatever the printing need. So what prevents you from running lots of 1,000 instead of 10,000? The answer almost always focuses on fixed setup costs versus variable costs. Where are the fixed costs in printing? Prep, plates, makeready time and makeready waste. If makereadies and setup waste can be reduced, the fixed costs are reduced. In fact, most digital presses have high variable costs and relatively low fixed costs, at least in comparison to conventional printing costs. We know that conventional presses with very short makereadies are very competitive against digital presses on short runs. Makereadies (fixed costs) can be reduced. Digital press speeds (variable costs) will increase. So, whether you are a digital printer or a conventional printer, you must keep improving. The marketplace will only get more competitive.

I know of companies who essentially contract with customers to offer fixed pricing for products regardless of the run length. In other words, a particular label costs $0.12 each whether you buy 500 or 50,000. How can that be? It may make sense on a digital press but how about a conventional flexo press? They can do it because they have reduced the vast majority of their fixed costs (makeready and makeready waste) so low that they do not substantially impact total cost. Customers love this type of pricing. Currently, there are still minimum orders (a certain number of feet of material, for example) but makeready is essentially taken out of the pricing equation. Why do these companies do this? Because they heard from their customers that they wanted flexibility on order quantity without having to pay premiums for short run lengths. They responded to their customer's value statement by focusing on reducing makereadies and increasing value creation activities.

Okay so Makereadies are BAD...Now What?

Well, that is why you've purchased this book. It isn't easy, but it is simple. The concepts are really quite basic and as much as anything you have to start with a fresh mindset and a fresh set of eyes when you approach your makereadies. This is a critical point of understanding. Everything you know about makereadies tells you they are part of printing. But you must change your mindset and agree that they need to be reduced substantially. In fact, you cannot simply work faster, nor do you want to; you must work differently. Rushing through your conventional process will only result in burned-out operators and lots of mistakes. So working faster is not the answer. Working smarter and working differently is the answer. Let us now start that journey. But before we do, we need to deal with some prerequisites; we need to get perspective by looking at the big picture.

What is your current view of makeready and how has it changed after considering value creation?

_____

_____

_____

_____

_____

_____

_____

_____

_____

_____

2 Lean Foundations: Creating a Competitive Advantage

The goal of every firm is to create a sustainable competitive advantage. How to best achieve this accounts for countless hours of management time and focus and can be the source of endless debate within company ranks. There are many pathways to success to choose from and a firm must choose carefully. Resources are always limited, capital is scarce and must be allocated appropriately, the environment you do business in changes rapidly, and competitive pressures only increase over time. Many companies choose to seek success through the implementation of Lean management principles. For those who select this route, this text will aid your journey.

Setup Reduction is rooted in Lean, and Lean management is fundamentally rooted in two basic principles: *Respect for People* and *Continuous Improvement*. These principles mutually support each other and are imperative for Lean to be successful within a company. Success in business does not come from taking short cuts, skipping steps in a process, or finding ways around basic principles. This also holds true for companies who wish to embark on the pathway of becoming Lean—it is important to understand the total commitment required to truly be Lean and not simply cherry pick the elements that seem appealing to you. Unfortunately, far too many printers have chosen to proclaim themselves proponents of Lean thinking without truly embracing the principles underlying Lean management. Will these printers improve? Possibly. Will their improvements be sustainable over time? Probably not. Would I want to compete against them if my firm really adopted Lean and was committed to Lean principles? Absolutely!

A neighbor of mine recently retired from a successful law practice. I saw him working in his garage one day so I stopped by to chat. He was doing some sort of household repair work and seemed to be thoroughly enjoying himself. As we chatted, one thing he said to me really stood out. He commented on how, now that he was not working full time, he had the time to "do things right." He was referencing the repair he was making but the comment was just as applicable to how many people and companies generally do business. Stopping to think about his remark I wondered how many times a printer rushes through a process or takes some sort of shortcut to quicken a project to completion.

In our working lives there never seems to be enough time to do it right the first time but always enough time to do it over if the job fails to meet some established criteria. Many of us have grown up in a corporate culture of conflicting priorities where we feel everything is important and we work from seemingly endless lists of things to correct, improve, maintain, look into, or resolve. Under the pressure to be seen as performing we adopt a general consensus that the greater number of things you can get checked off your list, the better. Employees are subtlety (and sometimes not so subtlety) guided to "do whatever it takes" to show progress on the issues at hand. This type of effort leads to a culture of motion, a culture of action (whether it adds any value or not), and a culture of rarely, if ever, fully resolving problems that do not reoccur. Despite valiant effort, seldom do these activities result in Setup Reduction.

Lean management is foundationally centered on the dual principles of *Continuous Improvement* and *Respect for People*. These two principles mutually support your efforts much like both of your legs support your body. Take away one of your legs and your ability to stand, walk, run, jump, or propel yourself suffers. Similarly, take away either of these principles and your ability to become Lean, and reduce setup time, is significantly crippled. Let us look at each of these in more detail.

Continuous Improvement

Continuous Improvement is easiest to address, as it is typically the concept that most printers can grasp quickly and feel they can enact with some speed. In Lean management, Continuous Improvement refers to the ongoing use of

Lean tools to reduce waste found in your business processes and to increase the value you provide to your customers.[1]

Lean businesses define value by understanding how, and what, their customers' value. If a customer does not value something it is considered waste and is targeted for elimination. Some waste may remain an integral part of your business due to a variety of constraints. These include the equipment you possess and its capabilities, your employees' abilities and understanding of Lean, your culture and its ability to modify and change, and your existing business processes and infrastructure. There is nothing wrong with calling things you currently do "waste." In fact, companies are encouraged to identify waste in their business even if they do not have a solution for minimizing or eliminating these areas. This is especially true in Setup Reduction, where you will regularly identify processes that aid makeready but should still be classified as waste, even if they are necessary and important today. Helping employees make the connection to know what the real waste in your organization is will help employees focus on finding the future means to reduce or eliminate it.

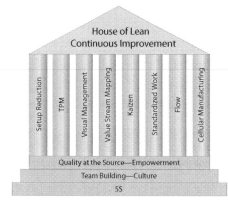

FIGURE 1: *Lean thinking is comprised of many principles and tools. Team building, empowerment, and 5s form its base. The many tools of Lean management are used to continually improve processes and systems.*

The Lean tools of Continuous Improvement include: Five S (5s), Total Productive Maintenance, Kaizen, the use of Flow, Kanbans, Cellular Manufacturing, Value Stream Mapping, Visual Management, and the focus of this book, Setup Reduction.

---

1   Illustration: Cooper, K., Keif, M. G., Macro, K. L. (2007). Lean Printing: Pathway to Success. Pittsburgh: PIA/GATF Press.

Respect for People

A key distinction separating firms in how they move along a Lean pathway lies in the second fundamental principle of Lean, *Respect for People*.

Respect for People is not clearly understood by many. If we were to ask the typical print shop owner if they respect their people, we would be surprised if many owners or managers would feel that they do not respect the people that work for them. The Lean principle of *Respect for People* goes far deeper than merely having some level of respect for your employees. In true Lean organizations, managers empower employees to enact change, improve processes, solve problems, and drive waste out of the organization. Employees drive change. Employees are the ones who identify waste, seek for new Setup Reduction techniques, and ultimate decrease setup costs. True Lean firms manage their culture with great forethought rather than putting all their emphasis on the implementation of Lean tools and letting the organizational culture evolve independently or as an afterthought.

> To encourage people to begin to think for themselves at work, get out of their way. Instead of telling people what to do when they ask, learn to ask them what they think should be done. It's truly amazing what can happen when you allow people to answer their own questions."
>
> — *LINDA HONOLD, FORMERLY OF JOHNSONVILLE FOODS*

One of the difficulties in embracing the *Respect for People* concept is that many aspects of embracing it entail the consumption of resources in the short-term. Empowering employees does not happen by merely stating your intention to do so, by announcing it at a plant meeting, or by creating a mission statement professing your respect for employees as an asset of the firm. Empowering your workforce means committing to training employees to work in teams, to learn problem solving processes, to creating an environment of continuous development, and being willing to commit to not laying off employees when improvements are made. Most, if not all, of these efforts can result in an increase in identifiable costs on your income statement.

What separates printers who only "do Lean" (and who do not find lasting benefit from their efforts) versus those who are "being Lean" is the commitment to employees by spending money to develop the workforce and the recognition that long-term value will be created from these efforts. For those who are beginning their Lean journey this requires some faith, as traditional measures of cost accounting view most employee-related activities as expenses and not as investments in the organization and its culture. You will save money with Setup Reduction, but there is an investment to achieving these savings—an investment in people.

Lean printers *involve* every employee. Each individual who works for you has the ability to improve your business. Management's role in a Lean organization is to embrace employee development, and employee empowerment, and to facilitate an environment of active problem solving and improving business processes. It is through recognizing the power of your company culture and actively managing this culture that enables a printer to become Lean. It is through people that Setup Reduction is significant and gains are made and sustained over the long-term.

Organizational cultures are created by leaders, and one of the most decisive functions of leadership may well be the creation, the management, and—if and when that may become necessary—the destruction of culture."

— EDGAR SCHEIN, PROFESSOR MIT
SLOAN SCHOOL OF MANAGEMENT

Managing and changing a company culture takes time and commitment. Improving your business through Lean principles is little different than raising a family. Bringing up children requires patience, a long-term view of their development, adherence to an established set of principles you value, and follow-through. Developing a strong family is not easy and neither is becoming Lean. When times are tough economically, parents still prioritize and find the means to develop their kids. Parents would not think of saying, "Well, we are having a tough quarter so there will not be food until the numbers improve." Companies must have this same mindset. Employees cannot be starved of training and development, or education, because the profit did not come in to expectation.

Change is hard and the more "seasoned" your press and bindery operators, the more reluctant they may be to change. If you jumped into Setup Reduction without an underlying culture for continuous improvement and change, you will see marginal improvements, followed quickly by setbacks. Change is only sustained when a culture of continuous improvement and Lean principles are well established in a company.

Many printing businesses today quite simply do not have the corporate value of continual learning and improving. They do not see themselves as a team of people who everyday look for new and better ways to grow in how they do business. Our system of promoting press operators promotes a sense of arrogance, not a sense of learning and sharing. Operators in many companies have "paid their dues" and don't want to work with others in continuing to improve as new concepts are discovered. This is a problem that must be addressed individually within each company.

But the problem does not lie exclusive with operators. Equally guilty, if not more so, are those managers who like to micromanage and do not give operators the opportunity to explore, learn, and innovate. Empowerment is critical to developing a solid Setup Reduction plan. Operators must be given the opportunity—no, the expectation—to revisit and explore their current procedures for setup. They need to have tools. They need to have training. They need to have resources. They need to have the freedom to explore without reprimand when a suggestion does not work. This is part of empowerment. Employees are given the power to change and improve their work processes. This allows many bright minds to engage in the improvement process rather than merely a couple of managers or supervisors.

Engaged operators and empowering managers are rare in the printing industry today. To be successful, your journey must start here. Without a culture of change and improvement you will fail at reducing makeready times. We have seen it happen too many times before. You need to start by focusing your employees on growth and improvement for the betterment of the business. If you are an owner, you may have some reluctant employees who think you are just trying to pocket more profit. But in this difficult business climate, it should not be a tough sell to focus on survival. Change is necessary to survive in the printing business. There is no question about it so conveying a sense of urgency should be easy.

With this urgency must come a genuine commitment to creating "something special." You truly do want to create a business that is responsive to customers and a world-class printing or packaging business. That may mean changing how you think and how you manage others. You will have to create a vision of what the organization needs to become. You will have to facilitate change by having a single, unified voice of what you are as an organization and where you are going. You will need to give up some control as you develop your people to lead in your Lean transformation. Lean principles are founded on the notion of discovery and improvement.

Toyota Production System: A Model for Setup Reduction

What made Toyota Motor Corporation the largest and most successful automobile manufacturer is more about their incredible commitment to continuously improve in all aspects of their business than about their equipment mix or their ability to hire the best operators. We know Toyota is not infallible. They lost focus (more than once) and have dealt with some bad press related to sudden acceleration and various other mishaps. They blew it and worked hard on getting refocused on customer value. We all agree brakes are valued and unintended sudden acceleration is not! Despite their setbacks, Toyota is a model for much of what we know about Lean and Setup Reduction.

Lean is a set of principles and values developed initially as the Toyota Production System (TPS) and later coined "Lean" by Womack, Jones, and Roos in their book *The Machine that Changed the World: The Story of Lean Production*. It was termed Lean because the system focuses on eliminating non-valued resources in production. Setup Reduction is a Lean principle. But it works best in concert with other Lean principles. So, in reality Setup Reduction is part of a larger management process and should really be treated as such.

Lean is a deep topic. Quite simply, it is one company's values, processes, tools, and metrics for making excellent products and providing valued services to their customers. Lean is a response to common business challenges.

You may wonder why we keep talking about a car company. What does Toyota have to do with printing and packaging? Well, Toyota has a very interesting history—one we can learn a great deal from. More importantly, they have addressed many of the same production problems you face and have developed innovative solutions to those problems. For many years Toyota was a small, family-owned business. The car company was a spin-off from the patriarch's loom business where he wanted to look at motorizing looms. Father Toyoda (yes, that is the correct family spelling) sent his son off to the University to study engines.

Toyota Motor Corporation was started right before World War II. Needless to say, their business timing was not great. After Japan was decimated by the war, the company struggled with poor sales, disgruntled employees, and strong global competition. The transportation infrastructure in Japan was in ruins and Toyota struggled looking for a market that was not shattered. They also needed to develop new methods to compete against much larger competitors, as Detroit's automotive success was setting their eyes on increasing market share abroad.

Those years were turbulent for Toyota. They had poor equipment, too many employees, and weak management. The president resigned in disgrace as the company struggled to stay alive.

Toyota knew their survival meant being responsive to customers so during the 1950's and 1960's they focused heavily on making cars—in very small lots. They had minimal production equipment to dedicate to different models. Detroit used single car lines for each model but the capital-constrained Toyota was forced to do elaborate changeovers for each car model. This was a big problem because the technology at the time required a 24-hour changeover to move from one car model to another. They needed a car line dedicated for each model or a car line that could be changed over in minutes but it simply was not financially feasible. Instead, they turned to SMED.

SMED

Single Minute Exchange of Dies (SMED) was developed by Shigeo Shingo, a consultant to Mazda, Mitsubishi (shipyard), Toyota and other Japanese manufacturers. SMED will be covered in great detail in the next chapter but what I want to convey here is Toyota's approach to the problem of long setup times. Common thought was that you leverage scale to be competitive. Detroit built big car lines and limited choice to consumers to keep costs down (think long press runs). They minimized downtime by limiting choice and pumping out mass quantities of identical cars. That was not an option for Toyota. Instead, they knew their customers valued choice. And their volume simply did not accommodate long production runs. Sound familiar? I bet many reading this text would fit into this camp too.

So what did Toyota do? They had two choices. They could try to emulate Detroit by focusing on economies of scale and standardized products. That would involve acquiring more equipment and dedicated production lines to single car models. This was the common thought of the time. Instead, they adopted a corporate model of value creation, questioning the status quo, and innovating to overcome current changeover problems. The operators were challenged to think beyond their current practices.

Shingo's outcome was spectacular. But don't be misled. It took time. There were challenges. It didn't all happen at once. But, Shingo was relentless in his pursuit of a vision to reduce changeover times to offer Toyota customers more value. He knew where Toyota needed to be so he kept the target in the sights of Toyota employees. They celebrated improvements but never quit looking to get better. This is the Toyota culture; it is the Toyota way. And don't be fooled by recent headlines. Toyota will learn from their mistakes and be back as the leading automobile producer in the world. Continuous improvement is entrenched in the Toyota corporate culture.

Lean is about seeing how you do business through new eyes. We get in patterns of doing things and without someone asking "why" on occasion, we never critically look at our processes. Lean is about asking "why". Lean is about defining customer value and then relentlessly pursuing methods to increase value creation and reduce non-value processes. It takes courage to ask "why", because sometimes we get married to those non-value processes. They define individuals and departments. Without focusing on the bigger picture—the customer—we can get stuck in protecting activities, even when they distract us from the better thing.

My first job in the printing industry was as an estimator for a commercial printing company. If I am a printing estimator, I certainly value its role in the company. I think it is important and I want to protect my job. But in truth, the process of cost estimating may not be something customers are delighted about paying for (e.g. not valued). It does not provide them directly with what they want: quality printed products. It may be a necessary activity, but it certainly is not what customers pay you to do. So, the healthier viewpoint is to call estimating what it is: a non-valued process or waste. And as such, we should focus our efforts into minimizing and streamlining the process so that more time and resources can be spent on value creation. If you are a skeptic by nature, you may say this is ridiculous. Estimators are not going to run out and operate a rewinder if we cut two hours out of their estimating schedule. But, that is exactly what Lean is about. Perhaps the estimator is not running equipment but there may be other activities that do involve value creation. Either way, Lean companies begin to look at things through the eyes of the customer. Doing so will make you invaluable to your clients. But it takes courage to take on this fresh approach.

A Lean culture takes time to develop. It cannot be rushed but it should involve urgency. As noted earlier, most employees are well aware of the competitive nature of print. Emphasizing the need for change and improvement is perfectly reasonable to most in the printing workforce. But, your actions must match your words. Don't talk about improvement and change if you intend on doing things as always from the corner office.

If you feel that you already possess a culture of change and improvement, then you are in a great position to move on with Lean principles. Lean is multifaceted. It is a subject that requires intense study and you will need to surround yourself with like-minded individuals.

5s

Lean may seem mysterious or even mythical. Many Lean concepts involve Japanese words. But in truth, the concepts are really quite simple. There are several tenants of Lean that work hand-in-hand with Setup Reduction including: 5s, Total Productive Maintenance, Kanbans, Kaizen, Flow, and Visual Management. You can learn more about these tools in other books. But one tool in particular is essential before starting a Setup Reduction plan: 5s.

5s is a tool popularized by Toyota for establishing an organized workplace. 5s is critical to enabling efficient production and rapid makereadies. It is essential to have a 5s workspace before attempting to undertake Setup Reduction. In fact, it is really important to achieve the fifth S, sustain, within a production space for an extended period of time before undertaking Setup Reduction. You will be asking operators to change. Initiating change is one thing but sustaining those same changes is quite another.

5s involves creating an organized workplace. It is a systematic process that focuses on how to best organize a space for maximum efficiency. It is a simple concept yet remarkably challenging to sustain over a period of time. As humans, we naturally clutter our workspace and hold onto things that are not essential for production but have some type of sentimental value to us. 5s is completely pragmatic. If a tool or supply has immediate value to the process, we keep it. As soon as it loses value, it goes. There is no room for sentimental connections in 5s.

There are five components of 5s. Since it was developed in Japan, The Five S's are Japanese words that translate loosely into five English words:

Seiri	Sort
Seiton	Set in order, straighten
Seiso	Shine or sweep
Seiketsu	Standardize
Shitsuke	Sustain

Lean principles are a dichotomy of *standardization with innovation*. While standardization and innovation seem contradictory, in truth they work well together. Employees are expected to be precise, exact, and conform to a standard. They are asked to understand the principles and focus on the objective—understanding value streams and ensure value creation is maximized. But, from there, they are asked to improve their process through continuous innovation. A common saying is "Nothing can be improved unless it is standardized." Standardization enables innovation, which then becomes the new standard, which further enables innovation.

Before you can focus on lowering your makeready time, you need to focus on "5s-ing" your work area. Do not attempt to reduce makeready times without first establishing a successful 5s initiative. Most Lean practitioners suggest starting with one production area, celebrating successes and building "islands of excellence." You want victories so you will need to lead the process, refocusing on the vision constantly. Management's new roll is casting vision, organizing training around this vision and ensuring the resources are there to accomplish the vision. Management must keep this vision in front of the organization constantly. It is very easy to lose focus when sales begin to lag or production difficulties arise. In fact, it has been well documented that companies often experience a drop in sales and profits before reaping the benefits of Lean.[2] It will happen. But, survival and increased profits are the long-term benefits of Lean and Setup Reduction.

> Islands of excellence means that a single system is optimized and proven before deploying across the company. Create your islands of excellence as a model for all to see and for which to aspire.

Using 5s as a backdrop for Setup Reduction is critical. Without a well-organized workspace, the operator is looking for the correct tool or supply when it is not returned to the correct location. Further, the operator is walking a distance to locate items because they are not in a strategic location. Clutter is the enemy of a quick makeready. Working around items or wading through to find the correct tool wastes valuable time. Excessive walking wastes time. 5s addresses these issues by placing all needed tools and supplies in strategic locations to minimize motion and delay. Let's examine each of the steps in more detail.

Seiri—Sort

Seiri is the first step of a 5s initiative. Seiri is necessary when beginning the process as most production areas have an excess of built-up clutter. Seiri involves sorting through all tools, supplies, benches, lighting, everything, all aspects of the work area, to remove items that are not immediately essential for production.

Consider all the things that have worked their way into the press area: sample wash-up solvent, sample plates or blankets, some old foil or lamination

---

2   Cooper R., Maskell B. (2008). How to Manage Through Worse-Before-Better. *MITSloan Management Review*, 49(4), 58-65.

material, bad stock that got shoved behind the delivery, dies and sheeters, a part from the press that was removed and is no longer used, an obsolete tool no longer used because of a press retrofit, and numerous other non-essential items.

Most companies choose to take a press, rewinder, or binder out of production for a brief period to jumpstart the 5s process. Sometimes the term "Kaizen" is used; a Japanese word that means continuous improvement. A Kaizen Event is an activity where a piece of production equipment is taken offline and a dedicated improvement process is initiated. A 5s Kaizen Event will take place over one to three days and will involve three or four people working diligently to identify those items that do not belong in the immediate area.

Most companies use a tagging system called "red tagging". Individuals go through the entire work area identifying items that should not be there. A red tag is put on the item. The tag signals to the team that the item is to be placed in a staging area for further analysis. The individuals are not identifying its final disposition at this point, just that it needs to be removed from the 5s work area (i.e. the press). Generally, another group will focus on the red-tagged staging area to determine what goes to long-term storage, what gets discarded, and what gets transferred to another area. Once the entire work area is sorted, it is time to start Seiton.

Seiton—Set in order, straighten

Seiton involves organizing the remaining items. At this stage, since many items have been removed, there is plenty of room to focus on the remaining items and where they should go. During seiton, we use the "three-easy" principle. We want the remaining tools, equipment, and supplies to be:

- Easy to see

- Easy to get

- Easy to put back

Seiton focuses on efficiency. In this process you should consider proximity to use. If a tool is used at the roll-stand, then it should be located at the roll stand, not the main console. Shadow boards are commonly used as a means to know where a tool goes and when it is missing. When possible, the shadow board should be within reach of its point of use. In other words, within five feet of where it will be used—within an arm's reach. Obviously safety issues or other motion and flow considerations may prevent that but since Setup Reduction is focused on reducing excess motion, placing shadow boards close to point of tool use is critical at this stage.

Focusing on material flow is important during Seiton too. Knowing that stock will be staged near the infeed portion of the press means that we need to consider material flow. Where will raw material come into the press production area? What will signal replenishment? (see Kanban, chapter 7) Where will finished goods go? How material flow works in production must be considered at all times.

Seiso—Shine or sweep

Cleanliness is an important part of 5s. Most pressrooms are not super clean. Many argue that presses just get dirty and we should not waste our time on shining a press. However, a clean work area instills exactness and attention to detail. Clean work areas help to remind all employees of the excellence that is performed in the company and the significance of precision machinery.

A clean work area also helps to immediately reveal problems. For example, if a press constantly has oil under the printing units, how will you know if you have a lubrication leak? If an ink fountain has ink all over it, how will you know if the ink leveler float is broken and ink is overflowing the fountain?

Seiso focuses on keeping a clean work area. This step is about making the area not only look good but also lint and dust free. Clutter not only attracts dust and the print defects that are associated with dust (pin-holes, hickeys, etc.) but it also impacts efficiency. Consider this: if you go into your neighbor's pantry to locate some pepper, how easy is it to find in a disorganized, cluttered pantry? Impossible. On the other hand, in a pressroom that is organized and clean, everyone can immediately locate tools and supplies when an immediate need arises.

Seiketsu—Standardize

Where is a commonly used tool like a plate wrench kept? The day shift operator keeps it on the workbench. The night operator keeps it next to the printing unit. And sometimes, both of them put it in their pockets. There is no standard location for the plate wrench so every day there is a brief period spent locating the tool. It may only be twenty seconds, but it happens day after day, week after week.

Standardization or Seiketsu is critical for Setup Reduction. Seiketsu in 5s is mostly focused on standardizing locations of tools and supplies and standardizing how the work area is maintained. It includes assessment and grading of 5s workstations. Standardization is a critical principle of all aspects of Lean and is particularly pivotal to reducing makeready time.

We often ask operators to work across different bindery lines or presses. Having standardized 5s work areas makes that process more seamless. However, one of

> Many companies use a peer-audit process to assess 5s work cells. Regular or random inspections are made by a peer group to help sustain the 5s work area.

the qualities Americans are particularly fond of is individuality. We want to show our uniqueness and how we do things different—better. While individuality can indeed be a great trait, it really does not work well in 5s or Setup Reduction. We are looking for standardization. Innovation has a place in Lean. As noted earlier, we are always focusing on improvement, but once something is improved, we are looking for standardization. And given two choices of equal strength and benefit...we pick one and ask all employees to adapt. This may appear to be a tough sell but when the common goal of creating value and eliminating waste is continually addressed, it is not as difficult as you imagine. You always come back to the goal: we are focused on value creation, what our customers want, and how we as an organization can develop to be the best printing company at providing valued products. It may take some self-sacrifice and swallowing of ego by all to achieve that goal. But, standardization is critical to achieving reduced makeready times.

Shitsuke—Sustain

The fifth stage is undoubtedly the most difficult—that is to sustain the improvements over an extended period of time. It takes discipline and focus. It is most natural for humans to revert to their previous practices and to clutter the area, slowing efficient makereadies.

So how do you sustain the 5s improvements already made? By revisiting the vision constantly. Without understanding why employees are being asked to keep an organized, tidy work area, they will grow bitter and resentful, as if their mother is asking them to keep their rooms clean. It is very important that this activity is not seen as a "big brother watching" scenario. When that occurs, then you will see scrambling to clean up when the boss is coming. That is definitely not what you want. You are looking to instill a new understanding of the benefit of an organized work area and providing the tools to achieve that goal. When company profits are reaped as a direct result of these efforts, employees engage, particularly when company profits translate into personal benefits like retaining a job, profit sharing, or even personal satisfaction of being involved in something bigger than oneself.

5s recognition is important. When high-levels are sustained, a team should be recognized and appropriately awarded. Even small recognitions go a long way to instill pride and motivate strong work cells.

Now that we have some understanding of the culture required for Setup Reduction and the infrastructure of 5s, we are ready to beginning addressing ways to reduce makereadies. There are two ways to approach this. One way is to work "faster". This is a mistake and will likely lead to safety problems. And while you likely can shave 10-20 percent off of your makeready times simply by working faster, you definitely will not be able to sustain those improvements over the long term. So you are better off approaching Setup Reduction a different way—approaching the problem in a completely unique manner. Only then will you be able to cut your makeready times in half and sustain those results over the long term. You can only achieve these improvements being Lean.

There is a significant difference between printers who implement Lean concepts by overlaying them on top of how they currently manage their business and those printers who truly redefine how they conduct business by embracing Lean principles. We define this difference as "Doing Lean" versus "Being Lean". "Doing Lean" will not lead to sustainable advantages and is akin to other "Flavor of the month" improvement initiatives that companies have tried before. No one should jump into Setup Reduction activities without

Doing Lean	Being Lean
Continues doing business the same way	Rethinks entire business and questions existing processes
Layers Lean tools on top of current processes	Company recognizes Lean is a philosophical direction to take entire business
Educates key plant leaders to run the process changes	Lean is seen as strategically important to long-term viability and success of firm
Lean is seen as a near-term improvement opportunity	Education is frequent, and constant, among employees and management
Lean momentum varies significantly within the plant and over time	Employees are empowered to make improvement to work processes
Lean proves difficult to sustain with old habits and work methods creeping back into use	Management supports Lean efforts with problem-solving tools and resources
Lean is viewed as an expense and is frequently cut when profit numbers do not meet expectations	Lean efforts do not diminish during tough economic times – rather these times reinforce the importance of becoming Lean
Management and employees not on the same page with direction and focus around Lean thinking	The use of Mission and Vision statements help to guide employees in making the best decisions

seriously considering broader Lean principles. Doing so will lead to frustration and unsustainable gains...at best.

This text will help you to understand what it truly means to become Lean in the print industry, how to reduce setup times, and avoid the common pitfalls that undermine printers' efforts to achieve their own Lean pathway to Setup Reduction.

How will your culture need to change to be successful at Setup Reduction? Where is your organization in terms of 5s?

_____

_____

_____

_____

_____

_____

_____

_____

_____

3 The Setup Reduction Process

Setup Reduction is exactly what it says: the reduction of setup or makeready time. It is more formally known as SMED, or *Single Minute Exchange of Dies* (see chapter 2). SMED focuses on identifying different makeready tasks and classifying them into internal or external operations. Internal operations are those tasks that *must* be completed while the equipment is stopped and external tasks are those that can be completed while the equipment is running. SMED also focuses on analyzing all tasks and figuring out ways to eliminate, reduce, or reengineer the task to shorten the time required to complete it. But before we get into those details, let us look more closely at the background of SMED.

You may recall that Toyota was a relatively small company in the 1950's looking to produce a variety of car choices with very little equipment. This is the same way most printers operate. Only a few of the very largest printers dedicate a specific press or binder to a specific product. Everyone else must change their folders, sheeters, binders, dies, substrates, rewinders, and ink systems daily for different products. These different components create value in the customer's mind but also require a changeover on the press. Toyota too adopted a practice of letting the customer determine the car model, colors, and options and the manufacturing line would adapt to fill the order.

You may ask: does Toyota really make a car to order? Don't they actually make cars and then have customers buy from inventory? In actuality, they do make cars to order. Toyota sells to the dealers based on custom orders. These Toyota dealers are in touch with their customers and buy models and features that they believe will be attractive for their clients. So they do manufacture to order—the dealers order. More importantly, when you see a Toyota manufacturing line, each car coming down it is different, they have found the means to mass-produce custom orders—this is the goal for any printer.

Now, back to the 1950's for a moment. As Toyota was trying to figure out how to work through this concept of variable product, they had a big obstacle to overcome. The die press required to stamp out car body parts required up to a 24-hour changeover time. This made it very difficult to produce different models without an elaborate changeover process, something they wanted to avoid.

The stamping dies weighed multiple tons and were very difficult to move. One of the reasons the stamping process was so time-consuming had to do with the way the dies were aligned in the stamping press. If not positioned to a tolerance of one millimeter, the output would contain defects. The process of registering the dies took multiple attempts and several hours of adjustment. In total, it took up to three shifts to complete a die changeover.

What would you do in this situation? Working faster simply would not provide the necessary improvements. Shingo, along with a number of Toyota employees, began to structurally analyze the setup process and identify steps necessary to fundamentally change the process. Change did not happen quickly. There were numerous setbacks but with time, they were able

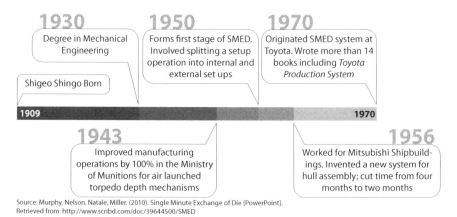

Source: Murphy, Nelson, Natale, Miller. (2010). Single Minute Exchange of Die [PowerPoint]. Retrieved from: http://www.scribd.com/doc/39644500/SMED

to reengineer the process from 24-hours down to 8-hours. From here, they worked through the process again and again over many years and got this same die change process to less than 10 minutes. Don't be fooled though.

It was a long, arduous process. Setup Reduction is a marathon, not a sprint. In fact, it is really not a race at all. It is a lifestyle commitment to driving out waste and optimizing customer value.

It may be important at this point to clarify that for the purpose of this book, we use makeready, setup, and changeover largely as interchangeable terms. Before you begin to focus on makeready or Setup Reduction, it is important to document your current makeready process and time. We will start there.

Where are you now?

How long does your makeready take for an "average" job? Thirty minutes, an hour, two hours? You need to have some good data as a baseline in order to know what is working and what is not. If you do not already have a means to gather makeready data, you need to start immediately.

Many companies use job tickets as a method to track makeready time. The operator logs the makeready start time, production start time, and the wash-up time. Others use data collection systems as part of a job costing MIS or CIM process. Either method is fine but the key is that we want to

MIS	Management Information System – an integrated database application with various modules including: estimating, order entry, inventory, job costing, etc. with the ability to generate real-time management reports.
CIM	Computer Integrated Manufacturing – Using computers to control the printing process. In particular, computers integrate the setup and feedback from equipment, typically using JDF.
JDF	Job Definition Format – JDF is a XML-based markup standard to speed production, increase reliability, and enhance the quality and flexibility of printed output. It was developed by Adobe as a nonproprietary standard.
CIP4	CIP4 is an international consortium of equipment suppliers who work together to develop standards to utilize JDF data to improve print automation.

know how long a makeready takes. If your job setups vary substantially by the type of job, it may be difficult to document an "average setup". If that is the case, you may want to classify your setups by category: one-color, process-color, converted product, gate-fold, and the like. It is important to have a well-documented benchmark to know if your improvement efforts are real and sustainable, or merely coincidental. When told that we are being analyzed, people naturally just work faster. But when you walk away, nothing has changed. Reliable data is important to assess your improvements.

What precisely do we want to benchmark? Initially, we would really like to know what happens during a shift. We ultimately need to know what happens during a makeready. But that will come later.

The Printing Industries of America (PIA) productivity benchmarks document averages for sheetfed offset printers. PIA documents four chargeable activities:

- Makeready

- Run time (and run speed)

- Wash-up

- Drying (sheetfed presses often have an offline drying [oxidation/ polymerization] requirement)

You will want to be as precise as you can in tracking these items. Obviously this list would look different for a flexo, gravure or web offset press and certainly there would be no drying requirement or wash-up requirement for most bindery equipment. Tailor your list to your specific equipment.

PIA also lists several typical non-chargeable items:

- Waiting for substrate

- Waiting for plates/cylinders

- Waiting for ink

- Waiting for customer

- Waiting for foreman/approval

- Waiting for repairs/maintenance

- Shift wash-up

- Routine maintenance

- Unplanned maintenance

- Repairs

- Re-work

...and about 30 other items that may potentially halt your production.

Since this book is focused on reducing makeready time, we want you to be certain you have tracked all activities related to makeready, but you certainly want to have a good handle on all activities that hinder maximum value creation for your customers. But we are getting a little ahead of ourselves. Let us get a bit more background on SMED. Then, we will cover techniques and methods to visualize and reduce makeready times in Chapter 4.

SMED Revisited

As noted earlier, SMED is a methodology for analyzing and reengineering equipment setup processes. Shingo wrote about SMED in several books, most notably *A Revolution in Manufacturing: The SMED System* (1985)[3] and *Quick*

---

3   Shingo, S. (1985). A Revolution in Manufacturing : The SMED System. New York: Productivity Press

Changeover for Operators: The SMED *System* (1996).[4] As noted earlier, Shingo, along with automotive employees, successfully converted a 24-hour setup process to less than 10 minutes using SMED techniques.

Using SMED, or what we are calling Setup Reduction, you can reengineer your makeready process and substantially take time out of setting up your binder, press, or rewinder. It will take some time to thoroughly analyze the process and generate viable solutions. In fact, it will take time to even see your problems. You need to come with fresh eyes to see where problems exist.

Cooperation among the various stakeholders in your business is essential. SMED works best with teams; involving a number of key individuals, both those familiar with the process and some who are not familiar with the process. Having "outsiders" is critical because they will ask the tough questions. They will ask, "Why do you have to do it that way?" "Why can't you do it this way?" These types of questions are important because you want everyone to look at alternative approaches to the makeready. You must begin to look at things differently—and remember that takes courage. And it takes courage to swallow one's ego and try something different, even though it has always been done a "certain way."

Let us now look at how you will reduce your makeready times. We have modified Shingo's original SMED process somewhat and organized it into ten steps. Each of these steps is explained in detail in the following chapters so if they seem vague now, do not worry. Just keep reading. The 10-step Setup Reduction Process for Print Manufacturing is:

1. Benchmark your current makeready

2. Minimize Internal processes

---

4   Shingo, S. (1996). Quick Changeover for Operators: The SMED System. New York: Productivity Press

3. Analyze, minimize, and standardize all setup tools and fasteners

4. Put tools and supplies close by and in an organized manner

5. Use positioning and registration aids to speed setup time

6. Work to minimize adjustment

7. Use parallel setup processes

8. Standardize, coordinate & improve your makeready

9. Mistake proof the process

10. When all else fails, reengineer the process

The Pit Crew Mindset

Before we go about the task of focusing in greater detail on these ten steps, I would like to briefly discuss the pit crew mentality. Makereadies are comparable to a NASCAR® pit crew (or select your favorite motorsport variety). As the driver pulls into the pits, the crew is focused and ready to take action. Immediately, seven pit members are over the wall and taking care of a well-choreographed, well-scripted changeover. Their actions in many ways will make or break the race that day. While the pit stop mentality is certainly not a perfect analogy to the bindery or press makeready, it has many parallels.

The biggest parallel is the urgency of reducing non-value time. Pit stops do little to create real value: completing laps and being the first over the finish line. They are necessary as they facilitate value creation but they are minimized so that the value-creation process is emphasized. Makereadies need to be minimized in order to maximize press and bindery running.

This requires preparation. Printers often do very little to focus on a quick changeover. How much time have you spent standardizing, scripting and choreographing your makeready? Treat it like a pit stop.

In *Circle Track* Magazine, there is an interesting article about what happens during a pit stop. Did you know that 19 operations happen in a NASCAR® pit stop? Did you know that one second saved in the pits equates to 279 feet of track position at 190 miles per hour?

> "When the car pits, two people stay on the inside of the wall, and seven others go over it and actually work on the car...The following is a basic four-tire and fuel pit stop, which took just 15 seconds and some change.

> "[The driver] must stop within inches of the markers in the pit so everybody can pounce on the car as planned. Seven crewmembers go over the wall, and two stay behind to provide assistance. Once the car is stopped, the gas can and the catch can go in the filler. The right side is worked on first; the jack man raises the car. Meanwhile, the windshield is cleaned (from behind the wall), and water is given to the driver.

> "Right-side wheel lug nuts are removed and the wheels are taken off. The tire carrier swaps the old wheels for new wheels, then cleans the grille (sometimes from behind, the wall). The right-side wheels are positioned, lug nuts get installed, and the jack man lowers the car.

> "The tire changers, the tire carriers, and the jack man sprint to the left side of the car. If anyone misses their mark, then chances are that someone will get plowed over by another crewmember. Meanwhile, more gas is needed, so another gas can is handed over the wall. The jack man raises the left side of car, and the left-side lug nuts are removed by the tire changers. Left-side wheels are removed, tire carriers swap old wheels for new ones, which are installed and tightened with lug nuts.

> "The gas can and catch can are removed, the jack goes down, and that's [the driver's] signal to let the clutch out and punch the gas.[5]

You've seen the same thing on television, haven't you? Have you given it much thought what they do during a pit stop? I find several interesting observations about this article. It is clear that someone has thought a great

5   Fitzsimmons, J. (2000) 15 Seconds. Circle Track, 19(6), 51.

deal about doing a pit stop...fast! Do we think about our makereadies that much? Do you study them and focus on how to shave another second off of them? Some may react to this article by expecting operators to run faster around the press during the makeready like a pit crew might. Sure, when you can safely do something faster, you should do it. But in truth, there are many, many things besides the pace of movement that are fundamentally different about a racing pit stop and the way you and I fuel and change tires on our car. It isn't merely that the pit crew is working faster than I work at home. They are working differently—fundamentally differently. They have different processes, different tools, different fasteners, different methods for adjusting, they have prepared things differently, and they have trained to be most efficient. They are working in parallel (as a team), they are minimizing their motion, and their technique is well developed.

In *Lean Printing: Pathway to Success* (2007) we quote another interesting article from *Circle Track* (2006) that details more of the preparation that goes into a pit stop:

> "One key to consistent pit stops is making sure the lug nut doesn't get stuck in the gun. Teams try to combat this problem with coated lug nuts. For many years, the lug nuts used throughout motorsports were plain steel. Recently, teams have wanted high visibility and slicker lug nuts, so a yellow Teflon coating has been added. They are lightly coated inside and out, which provides a cleaner release from the socket and lubrication onto the studs.

> "Once the nut is on the stud, the key is to get it smoothly down the threads. Some teams are using [an] anti-seize/Ballistol® mixture on the threads themselves. This again provides smooth lubrication on the threads to reduce the torque required from the impact wrench. This has reduced the time hitting the lugs 25 to 40 percent by some estimates. Another benefit to these mixtures is their ability to reduce the sticking of the lug nut glue to the threads of the stud.

"The guns used on pit stops are not your average impact wrenches. They are custom tailored to quick pit stops. These guns, depending on manufacturer, can cost from $800 to $1,300.[6]

Let us consider some of the key elements of a typical pit stop in light of the Setup Reduction process. It is clear from this article that focusing on tools and fasteners is essential for a quick pit stop. It is also essential for a quick makeready. Clearly the race is won or lost based on how well the tools operate, how the materials are prepared, how the fasteners are lubricated, and how standardized the pit process is so that it can be repeated each and every time with no flaws.

While it is not explicit in these articles, positioning aids are used to help the lug nuts go on correctly the first time. By gluing the lug nuts in position on the wheel prior to mounting the wheel on the car, all five lug nuts can be tightened in less than three seconds. Using torque impact guns, there is no adjustment required once the lug nuts are tightened.

The pit crew is a team. They work hard to standardize everyone's role and ensure the process goes smoothly. Trent Cherry, coach for the Penske Racing pit crews stated, "I don't want seven all-stars, I want seven guys who work as a team." (St. John, 2008)[7] The pit crew uses parallel procedures. They have seven individuals over the wall working parallel steps to reduce the time in pits to fewer than 15 seconds. Certainly one individual could never do all that is necessary in that short a time, and probably not in seven times that length of time.

Most importantly, pit teams study and then they practice. They standardize the process and they improve it. They focus on critical roles. Who is responsible for what? What tools are needed? What can be prepared ahead

---

6   Whitney, M. (2006) Quick pit stops: some little-known elements make a big difference. Circle Track, 25(1), 72-77.

7   St. John, A. (2008, May 9). Racing's Fastest Pit Crew. The Wall Street Journal [On-line]. Available: http://online.wsj.com/article/SB121029940935779803.html [2009, July 7].

of time? How can they maximize efficiency in the pits? They use many Setup Reduction principles during their brief changeover. Your goal is to use those same Setup Reduction principles to focus on improving your setup time… substantially. Not by working faster, but by working differently. Continual education of your team members is a big part of Setup Reduction.

Your Setup Reduction Team

To start on your journey to reduce makereadies, you'll want to assemble a team—your Setup Reduction team. This will be a group of several interested individuals who will work through the Setup Reduction process to identify bottlenecks, improve the work area, and focus on reducing setup time. Team member selection is important, as you'll want to have a group who will work well together and have a vision for what can be achieved. They will also need to study the process and meticulously analyze the existing

> **Developing Strong Teams**
>
> High performing teams have the following characteristics:
>
> - Clear sense of purpose and mission, shared values
> - Strong communication skills
> - Effective conflict management and time management tools
> - Empowerment to act on ideas
> - Support of management with resources
> - Commitment to succeed

makeready practices. Big egos may struggle as team members, so keep that in mind as you assemble the team. When questioning procedures, nothing is off limits. Everything is questioned and no creative ideas are discounted until they have been thoroughly considered. Basics of team dynamics: respect, trust, openness, listening, commitment, vision, and brainstorming, are needed for effective outcomes.

You will want to make sure you do not tackle too much initially. Many setup initiatives have failed by not controlling the pace of the initial efforts. We recommend you start with just one area and develop some success before trying to take on your whole pressroom. Develop *islands of excellence;* model Setup Reduction cells that serve to inspire future improvements. You'll want to select one work area to start, ensure success, and sustain the improvements before institutionalizing the process. You'll need to do lots of training before and during your Setup Reduction. Give employees this book, conduct internal training, or bring in a consultant to help jumpstart your efforts. But one way or the other, show your commitment through lots of training, and a consistent vision and constancy of purpose.

Your team will likely include a couple of operators, possibly a supervisor, and likely one or two individuals from outside the work area. These "outsiders" are important and should be empowered to speak up and ask questions. Outsiders are not "indoctrinated" and therefore ask those important "hard questions." Make sure that your team understands the value of these individuals. They are key members and deserve to be listened too. It helps when the outsider(s) have a keen sense of group dynamics and the ability to communicate tactfully.

Your Setup Reduction team will be responsible for all phases of the Setup Reduction process. They will review video of existing makereadies. They will identify and categorize makeready activities. They will use 5s concepts to analyze and reorganize the work area (5s should be done prior to Setup Reduction). The team will look for ways to reduce and standardize fasteners and tools. They will analyze the way the makeready is performed: the sequence, whether activities can be done in parallel, and how adjustments can be minimized to speed up the setup.

The next several chapters breakdown the Setup Reduction process into smaller chunks. Our goal is to give you the tools so that you can analyze and improve your own makeready. No two presses are identical and no operators work the same, at least instinctively. There are no shortcuts for Setup Reduction. You must work through the process to improve. This is one of those activities where the *means* is critical to the *end*. Don't try to cut corners or speed up the process by using an expert or consultant for driving the change. Consultants can jumpstart the process, coach, and help with training, but this is about your operators learning to see inefficiencies. It is vital that your team own the Setup Reduction process. It is a bottom up improvement process, not top down. So refrain from controlling the progress. Your job is to train and provide resources. Now, let's get this started!

How does your company currently approach makereadies? How do you see adopting a pit crew mentality could change your approach to makereadies?

_____

_____

_____

_____

_____

_____

_____

_____

_____

4 Benchmarking your Current Makeready

The first step of the Setup Reduction process is to identify and document setup activities by listing and classifying each task as either an *internal* or *external* activity. An internal activity is one where the machinery is idle (stopped) as the setup activity is performed. For example, when you mount plates, the press is stopped. When you change the gate position on a folder, the folder is stopped. When you change a rotary die on a label press, the press is stopped.

An external activity is one that is completed while the equipment is in operation. This includes numerous items including staging stock, reloading inks (in most cases), setting impression, reading job tickets, and the like.

There are lots of printing presses and finishing equipment out there: flexo, offset, inkjet, stitchers, folders, etc. Each has its own requirement and each makeready is done differently. What may be an external operation on one press is an internal operation on another one. So, if you read something in this text that does not make sense for your equipment, just grasp the concept and apply it in the correct method within your environment.

Your goal in the first step of the process is to focus on what you are doing today. Before you begin to improve the process we want to document today's "norm". We are benchmarking. The goal is to observe, document, and categorize. Do not look to improve just yet; that will be difficult to refrain from when you start to really "see" inefficiencies.

Learning to observe may take practice. Have you ever noticed how messy your garage is? We become blind to our own "stuff". But when you go see your neighbor's garage, it is obvious that he has a lot of clutter. It is only when we take a step back and really look—with fresh eyes—that we see the problems. Learning to ignore what "we know" in exchange for of seeing what is really happening, is a challenge. Your operators may struggle with this too. They have been doing their jobs in some cases for twenty or thirty years. They already "know" what is happening. They may be reluctant to look with fresh eyes because it may seem demeaning. In truth, it is natural to become immune to inefficiencies. You can see why training, combined with frank discussions and a clear vision, is vital for success. Having a facilitator or coach as part of the team may help to calm nerves and encourage deeper understanding.

So, how are you going to accomplish this benchmarking? Some people call this *current state* documentation. The premise is that you are documenting how it is done today—the current state. When discussing the point when efficiencies are improved, we call that a *future state*.

The best way to document the current state is to actually watch and video every makeready step as it happens. This needs to be done for an "average" makeready. Since there are so few "average" makereadies in many printing environments, you may need to review multiple makereadies and calculate some average times.

Video and Spaghetti Mapping

The best way to benchmark current setup practices is by videoing and analyzing a makeready. The advantage of videoing is multifaceted. First, if you get the camera far enough away, you will not have operators acting "differently" for the camera. The goal is to get a realistic perspective of the day to day. Put the camera up in a loft, suspend if from the ceiling, or simply place it far away from the press. The objective is to get a very broad view of the work area. You need it close enough to be able to tell what an activity is but far enough away to see the entire press and the movement involved during a makeready. I recommend sticking it on a tripod to avoid too much interference and distraction from the camera. This is not about good video quality; it is about being a "fly on the wall."

The second advantage of videoing is the ability to stop and start the video during analysis. This is necessary because the goal is to identify activities performed and time their duration. Having a pause button really makes this simple.

Perhaps the most compelling reason to video is to allow operators to see themselves during a makeready. This is powerful. Ask an operator how long it takes him to mount a plate and you'll get an answer. Then watch it with him using a stopwatch and you may find out that in reality, it takes much longer (or shorter) than the operator initially thought. This gets back to the point of focusing on real, documented activities. We all have perceptions that do not match precisely with reality. That is normal. But, we want to focus on reality here and videos do not lie.

Try to be unobtrusive with the video so that your employees act as naturally as possible. Once they know the ultimate use of the video, they will begin to feel more comfortable with the camera and eventually forget it is even there. In the end, they will use the video as a resource for improving their makereadies. It is not a tool for performance evaluation or critique (other than self-critique or peer-critique). It is a resource for professional growth and is used for self-assessment. That is important for them to know.

Once a makeready video has been captured, you will want the team to sit down and analyze it. There are a number of ways to do this but my preference is to have three items handy:

- Press diagram (low detail schematic or outline)

- Activity log

- Stopwatch

The press diagram is used for what is called *spaghetti mapping*. Spaghetti mapping is a tool for documenting movement around the press. The press diagram should be very low detail and basically show the press footprint and surrounding work area. It can be hand drawn if necessary. It is called a spaghetti map for obvious reasons…it looks like a bowl of spaghetti in most circumstances.

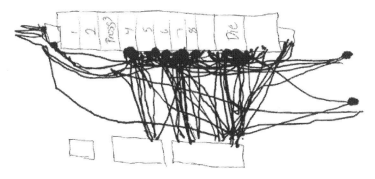

FIGURE 2: *An example of a spaghetti diagram*

The spaghetti map really does not provide a lot of detail. It merely provides a visual representation of operator movement. And motion takes time. Remember the pit crew and how focused they were on minimizing motion? Makeready motion increases setup time. Every time someone walks to the delivery to pick up a tool for use on the feeder, valuable time is consumed… maybe only a few seconds but seconds add up when repeated throughout a shift.

The spaghetti map gives us a visual representation of what is happening and when repeated after implementing Setup Reduction, shows us improvements that are made. We assume that the bowl of spaghetti is going to get a lot smaller once we implement many of the Setup Reduction strategies. Operator movement is decreased so the complexity of the map and volume of lines are decreased. And that is the goal: reduce the amount of spaghetti.

How does one complete a spaghetti map? Well it is very simple. As you watch the video, you simply draw the movement of the operator around the work area. As the operator goes to the delivery, your pencil line goes to the delivery. As the operator goes to the ink cabinet, the pencil line goes to the ink cabinet. As the operator walks to grab a plate, the pencil line goes to the plates. Initially, you will want to have a separate diagram for each operator but at some point, the amount of movement may be minimized to the point where you can put two or more operators on a single sheet, perhaps using different colors of pencil.

This tool is a visual tool and while it is very impactful (visual things usually are), it doesn't truly provide a lot of data points. For that, you will need to get your activity log and stopwatch.

Setup Activity Log

The activity log is your place for identifying and categorizing each makeready activity for your current state. Using a stopwatch, your team will focus on one operator at a time (or you can have two members of your team focused on one operator and two members focused on a second operator). Working in 15-second segments, write down what the operator is doing. You'll have to start and stop the video often. But then again, that *is* why you taped it. If there are four different activities going on in that 15-second time period, write down all four items. Beside each item, write the duration of the task as well as the accumulated time for the task. Your primary objective is to document every minor detail of a typical makeready as you doing it today—in the current state.

One question that comes up is what unit of time do you use during benchmarking: seconds or minutes. It is your option but minutes, and portions of minutes, usually works best at this phase. So, if an activity takes 75 seconds, simply record 1.25 minutes. When you get to where your makereadies are really fast, you may choose to switch to using seconds.

As you write down a task and record its duration, determine if the equipment is running or not at the time the task is performed. By running, I really mean producing product. In other words, if the activity is completed while the

Machine:
Crew:
Operator:

Tools:

Date:
Job Details:

Current State Documentation

Task No.	Elapsed Time	Task Time	Task/Operation title (include idle time)	Benchmark			Future State Analysis — Observations/ Improvement suggestions	Target Time		
				Equip. running? (√ if applies)	Equip. stopped? (√ if applies)	Parallel with operator/ task...		External (run)	Internal (stop)	Parallel with operator/ task...
1										
2										
3										
4										
5										
6										
7										
8										
9										
10										
11										
12										
13										
14										
15										

previous job is still running, check the *equipment running* cell, if not, check the *equipment stopped* cell. Finally, indicate if any tasks are performed in parallel with other operators.

If you look at the sample activity log provided, you'll notice that I include a portion for current state documentation and a section for future state analysis. You may want to separate the two and create another form. This log is a bit crowded but I like having the analysis side by side with the current state documentation. Either way, make sure you create a copy of the current state documentation without the analysis included so you have a clean baseline to reference back to.

You do not want to rush the documentation time. Let your team discuss what is happening on the video. Let them write their observations. One key disadvantage to having the future state analysis right there with the documentation is that team members may be tempted to "improve" too early. The goal is simply to document and analyzing too early may result in inaccuracies or presumptions. There is a place where observations and suggestions can be written. Writing ideas may be included along with the documentation phase. In fact, it is a good place to jot down some brainstorming ideas so they won't get lost. But, be cautious about jumping to the strategy phase too early.

Benchmarking Steps

1. Video a current makeready
2. Analyze by completing activity log
3. Spaghetti map each operator
4. Future state analysis

In most cases, you can document a one-hour makeready in a day or less. It doesn't require a lot of thought but it is important that the Setup Reduction team (and particularly the equipment operators) be the ones doing the documentation. The last thing you want is to have an operator questioning the accuracy of the current state documentation. Once they do it, they have *seen* with their own eyes the realities of the makeready and agreed that the documentation is accurate. When you are satisfied that all makeready tasks have been accurately documented, you will be ready for analysis.

Future State Analysis

Now that you have a solid understanding of where your process currently stands, you can begin to improve the process. Remember, it is a ten-step process and we are only on step one. Each step offers small, but substantive improvements. Do not expect any one step to give you radical improvements but when combined, their effect is dramatic.

During the analysis, you want to have your team brainstorm. This is where your "outsiders" will earn their pay. As the team begins to discuss each task in a makeready, several key questions are asked:

- Is this task necessary? If the answer is no, get rid of it now.

- Must this task be an internal operation (must the equipment be stopped)? Often safety concerns dictate an internal operation, but now is the time to start asking the hard question.

- What would need to change to make it in external operation?

If it can be changed to external, write down the external target time for that task. If it cannot be changed, write down the internal target time for that task. We will discuss this concept more in the next chapter.

- Which tasks could be done in parallel with other tasks? Are additional resources needed (more personnel) to accomplish that?

- What other suggestions or observations can you provide to speed setup time?

There is a high likelihood that friction may occur during these discussions. The equipment operators will want to defend their practices. The outsiders will (hopefully) challenge those practices and make the operators defend their practice and provide strong rationale. If the team has been trained well, this conflict can be very helpful. The key is managing egos. Nobody wants to look dumb or incompetent. It is natural for the operator to either feel wrongly judged or stupid for not seeing inefficiencies earlier. Helping to manage these emotions may be necessary. The stronger your work culture is (trust) and the more tactful team members are (respect), the easier the process is.

When you have completed going through each operator's makeready tasks and looked at alternatives, your team may want to implement some solutions. Let them go for it. It is common to see 10-20% improvement in setup time simply by watching, documenting and analyzing current states. However, do not confuse exuberance with sustainable improvements. If you have done your job in training and coaching you will have some excited employees. That is great. Their eyes will be opened to new ways to do things, simply by watching themselves—much like professional athletes improve by watching their batting motion or golf swing. However, you will need to standardize and institutionalize your improvements before you can expect long-term benefits. That will come soon.

What do you anticipate "seeing" when you benchmark your current makeready?

5 Minimize Internal Processes

Improving makeready time involves ensuring that all external activities are actually completed while the previous job is still running. The idea of separating activities into the two categories helps us to identify the minimum time needed for a makeready without reengineering, using parallel processes, or otherwise improving each setup task. In other words, without actually changing anything other than *when* a task is done, I can add up the total duration of internal setup tasks and know the minimum time required for a makeready. We still want to improve processes but for the moment, let us assume that our sole goal is to change *when* a task is done, not how it is done. The primary question then is simple: are those tasks that can be done while the equipment is running actually being completed before the prior job is finished? Stated another way: when the press stops, are there any makeready tasks that are being performed that could be performed externally?

Let us walk through an example. I am going to use a flexo label press for illustrating the concept but any printing, converting, or binding equipment would work. What are the discrete steps that a single press operator on a small label press would go through during a makeready?

External	Internal
Making plates	Stock loading on roll-stand(s)
Read job ticket	Ink loaded
Stage stock	Cylinders mounted/preregistered
Stage ink	Aniloxes mounted
Stage plates	Impression setting
Stage other (cores, lamination, etc.)	Die mounted/preregistered
Locate tooling (dies, etc.)	Plate/die registration
Plate mounting*	Adjusting inks
	Color match (approval)

*Flexo usually mounts to cylinders offline, offset includes punching plates

While this list may not be comprehensive, it does touch on many of the typical makeready functions. Normally these tasks would be listed and then I would go back and categorize them but I am going to show it here already categorized. For now, I am not going to worry about times, just the activities.

If you run flexo label presses you may be able to expand this list immensely. But, assuming for the moment that this is a relatively accurate list, and assuming that you agree on the categories selected, what processes need to be in place to ensure that the external activities are completed *before* this job makes it to press? Well, obviously, the operator needs to have the job ticket and have the availability to read it while the previous job is wrapping up. Are you prepared to have their attention taken away while the previous job is finishing running? That may be dangerous! But, before you throw the idea out, what would it take to make this a reality? Would another operator need to watch the job? Could there be a roving operator (like a makeready expert) that could show up ten minutes before a job is complete to initiate this task? This is where the creativity of your Setup Reduction team comes in handy.

Okay, what about staging stocks, inks, supplies, plates and other items. Who will do that? Are you prepared for your operator to leave the press and gather those items? Perhaps you already have a staging system in place with another employee but if not, now is the time to consider how to do that. Again, using the makeready assistant concept, how about having someone prepare all materials ahead of time and have them staged in the correct location upon shutdown of the previous job.

You get the idea, no doubt. The first step after completing your analysis is to really focus on those tasks you agree *could* be done externally if planned for. Now, you just need to get your team to do the planning. You will need a way to signal or a way to predict when a changeover will start. If a task can be done externally, then make sure it is done externally. Talk through each item on your makeready activity log so that anything that says "external" is thoroughly addressed.

Converting Internal to External

There is a second factor to consider in this Setup Reduction step. Can internal tasks be converting into external tasks? The short answer is "often." The longer answer is that it may take significant reengineering and it may take money. But, do not give up too easily here. We will talk about reengineering later in the book, but for now, let us keep it simple. So the question stands: can any tasks be converted from internal to external without reengineering the task?

I would be remiss if I led you to believe that you can always convert a makeready task from internal to external. It simply cannot always be done. You are not likely going to be able to change an offset printing blanket while the previous job is running. Safety and the simple realities of physics make the process unlikely at best and probably impossible. But, that does not mean you do not ask the hard questions. What would need to happen to move this task to an external task? Once that question has been thoroughly considered do you move on.

Looking at the previous list of internal activities, this is what we came up with:

Now, of these internal tasks, are there any that could be converted in part or in its entirety to an external process. I see three that show some promise: Loading ink, setting impression, and adjusting inks. Now, don't quit on me. I am not saying I can walk

Internal
Stock loading on roll-stand(s)
Ink loaded
Cylinders mounted/preregistered
Aniloxes mounted
Impression setting
Die mounted/preregistered
Plate/die registration
Adjusting inks
Color match (approval)

into your shop and magically make these external. What I am saying is that with some thought, there may be portions of these tasks that could be done externally. Hear me out.

Starting with loading inks. Flexo label presses (I realize other presses are different) often have removable ink pans or fountains. Because of this, it may be possible to own multiple sets and use a set to preload inks, in which case the pan is mounted ready to go. Yes, you'd have to consider how to do it without spilling but think of the timesavings over the hundreds of jobs that are produced in a year on this label press. Now, if this does not seem like a reality to you, fine. But do not check out or give up. Grasp the principle. The goal here is to get the creative juices flowing. The savvy Setup Reduction team listens, chews on the concepts a bit, and then comes up with clever ideas. If they do not work, you do not stop coming up with clever ideas, you just move on.

Now, let us talk about setting impression. Depending on the flexo press, impression settings may vary dramatically with repeat size (cylinder circumference), plate relief, and substrate. But, impression settings are often more a function of stock variation than cylinder size or plate relief. So, doing a quick presetting during the conclusion of the previous job may not be impossible. Especially if you know that you can fine-tune the setting upon start-up. In this situation, a portion of the task may be taken offline.

Ink adjustments are a classic for the flexo label printer. The inks are toned during the color match process using ink colorants to get that perfect spot color. This seems like a natural to move to external operation. The cynics out there will say, "The proofing tools aren't good enough and I will still have to adjust on press." Well, ink proofing tools are getting very good. And if you control your processes well, you might find that you can do external

Low-hanging fruit External Tasks

Staging stock and inks

Reading job tickets

Acquiring dies

Retrieving plates

ink color adjustments with precision. Put your brightest and best color operators on the task and you may find out you have moved that function entirely external.

So, the question of *when* to complete a task is an important one. The norm is to not do anything until the previous job is completed. Then we start to think about the next one. But, a key way to reduce your makeready time is to devise a system that maximizes external tasks—sometimes called *premakeready*. It is unlikely that a single operator can do it all. You'll need to look at your staffing and see if you can free someone else up. Many presses have two operators. But during the run period, especially after it has been running well for a while, that second operator may be freed-up to begin the premakeready of the next job.

One final thought…it is too easy to simply say, "You can't convert that task to external." When I work directly with teams, I always encourage them to ask, "Why can't it be external?" Or, "What would it take to make it safe to do externally?" The trick is not to give in too easily to the notion that we must do things the way we always have.

Let me conclude this chapter by discussing a challenging internal task from my previous list, perhaps mounting plate cylinders in the press. Everyone would conclude that the safety risk of trying to mount a cylinder on a moving press would be astronomical. Only a naive (and dangerous) employee would try such an endeavor. But, before I walk away from this, I am going ask the question, "Why?" Safety. Fair enough. But, what would it take for me to be able to mount a cylinder on a moving press? That question is where you begin to brainstorm. If it were a servo press, could I disengage one unit while the others are still printing? Could I mount a plate onto a device that then loads it on the fly (offset presses already do this)? Some manufacturers are addressing these challenges in their new press designs today. Someone must recognize existing process steps as waste before change occurs. Identifying waste gives you a new perspective when looking at reengineering options or when looking at acquiring new equipment. So, when you ask these questions, ask them to equipment manufacturers too. Why? So they know it is important. Do not skip the asking and addressing of hard questions. It is simply too easy to dismiss things without giving them adequate thought.

Question Everything.

As you think about your current makeready, what are some internal tasks that could be moved to external tasks?

_____

_____

_____

_____

_____

_____

_____

_____

_____

6 Analyze, Minimize, and Standardize All Setup Tools and Fasteners

The third step of the Setup Reduction process involves looking carefully at your tools, bolts, nuts, and other fasteners. A great deal of time is spent working with tools and fasteners during the setup process. Most press and bindery equipment comes with tens if not hundreds of fastener styles and dozens of tools. Each time you mount a plate, you use a plate wrench to open clamps (offset). Each time you rotate cylinders, you use some type of gear wrench (offset). Each time you adjust your trucks in a die station, you use a particular allen wrench or hex key (flexo). There are many sizes of wrenches, screwdrivers, and specialized tools used in most modern presses, rewinders, and finishing equipment.

The typical manufacturer considers a number of structural factors when selecting a bolt, thread engagement, washer and nut. Since I am not a mechanical engineer, I will not attempt to address design requirements related to shear and tensile stress for a given application. I'll leave that for the engineers. But, what I can comment on is that the bolt type, thread engagement, and overall fastener efficiency for operators is critical. Lean equipment design considers how the operator will use a fastener.

Let me ask a simple question? Why does a binder or press need twelve different bolt head styles or sizes? Why not one or two sizes and one or two wrenches? In many cases, the answer lies more with what is readily available to the engineers than what is easiest for making quick adjustments. Fortunately, many of these fasteners can actually be swapped out without compromising the integrity of the bolt or the component the bolt is fastening. Better yet, make your buying decisions contingent on equipment designed for quick changeovers.

Let us review what the purpose of a fastener is. Obviously, the goal is to secure something in place so that the equipment can function properly.

Structural engineering principles dictate the size, engagement, and grade of a fastener. Obviously press and binders running at high speeds have tremendous stress loads and vibration. However, the stress load usually has minimal influence on the style or size of the fastening head. Torque requirements for tightening the fastener may, so there certainly could be an argument for a few different sizes and styles for high-torque applications. But in general, many fasteners could use the same head regardless of size and thread engagement. This principle will speed the setup time by minimizing the different types of tools needed. When possible, head styles and sizes should be minimized and standardized. Changing your equipment to fasteners with common style and head sizes is something equipment team members can readily do and will likely give them a sense of satisfaction in making progress on reducing setup times.

Common Types of Fasteners

There are number of common fasteners we see on presses and binders. Among the common types are: Screws; Bolts, Nuts, and Washers; and other fasteners.

Screws

Screws are used with threaded holes. Bolts are used with nuts. There are numerous scenarios on presses where screws are used to fasten components. It could be a die bridge, doctor blade holders, a cleanup blade, or a pocket of a binder. In situations where a screw is used, consider using a convenient and standard head style and size, so that only a few drivers are needed.

Bolts, Nuts, and Washers

Bolts are used with washers and nuts. Whenever there are multiple components to a fastener, it will slow the operator down substantially. The nut falls on the floor. The washer is installed backwards. The washer falls off. For these reasons, it is preferable to not use bolts and nuts when a screw and threaded hole is an option. Using screws with built-in lock washers is also preferred to minimize miscues. In nearly all cases, replacing loose washers with built-in washers is easily done.

Other Fasteners

There are many other fasteners including cotter pins, keys, and rings. Each should be examined and alternatives considered. A critical eye needs to examine all fasteners and consider alternatives that will minimize handling and adjustment time while not impacting structural integrity.

Head Styles—Drives

Screws and bolts can be tightened with many types of wrenches including conventional closed or box-end hex wrenches, Allen wrenches, Torx wrenches, and various other styles. Torque wrenches help to ensure that a bolt or screw is tightened sufficiently without over tightening. Select the correct wrench for the job and standardize. Under few circumstances (as in never) should an adjustable wrench be used on the factory floor. While flexible, they take far too long to adjust and do not retain a tight fit during an adjustment. So, get rid of your adjustable wrench in the pressroom. Go out and buy good quality drives.

Slotted and Philips drives are rarely preferred for mechanical adjustments. They are slow and strip easily. More common for industrial equipment are hex drives, hex sockets (Allen), and Torx drives. Observation (study your video) will immediately tell you if your operators are struggling with a fastener. Can you loosen the screw in one second? Can it be retightened in one second? Is it lubricated enough to tighten without binding? Can the wrench be engaged quickly and stay on during the operation or does it slip on and off. These are the questions to determine if you are using the right drive.

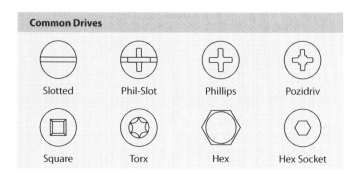

Common Drives

Slotted	Phil-Slot	Phillips	Pozidriv
Square	Torx	Hex	Hex Socket

Quick Release and One-Turn Fasteners

The goal of examining fasteners is to focus on reducing the time it takes to make an adjustment and to ensure that the adjustment is done in one quick motion. Often, operators spend valuable time turning a screw repeatedly to disengage it for an adjustment. We want to look to strategies that allow the operator to loosen the screw or bolt in one turn, make the adjustment and then tighten in one turn to complete the operation. Conventional fasteners rarely offer such benefits. So, consult local sources to see if quick release or one-turn fasteners are available.

Quick release can be achieved in a couple of ways. A common way is to make the threaded nut expandable to release the screw. RotoMetrics, a St. Louis based rotary die and accessory manufacturer makes a die bridge with a cam lock that engages the inner threads of the nut. The screws allow for hundreds of pounds a pressure to be applied to a die. When the cam lock is disengaged, the twelve-inch screws slip out for quick adjustments to other die sizes. This simple retrofit can save 2-5 minutes per changeover simply in turning the long screws that came standard on the press.

Whenever you see someone turning a screw or bolt for more than a revolution or two, you must ask yourself if there an alternative. Is a quick release alternative commercially available or is a custom retrofit possible. The economics almost always make sense—one can easily do the math. If a press hourly rate is $250, then two minutes costs about $8.30. So, how many two minute time chunks are wasted by poorly designed screws and bolts? If you can eliminate three of those per shift, you can afford $13,000 in retrofits and still have a 1-year ROI (assuming two shifts, five days). The numbers really add up.

Remember to consult an engineer to ensure you are not sacrificing structural integrity whenever you retrofit fasteners. You don't want to short-bolt a component. However, you may be able to increase a screw's length of engagement to compensate for any structural concerns related to changing to a quick-release fastener.

Take this seriously. When you evaluate your video, look for areas where you see an operator adjusting a screw or bolt. Attack those areas aggressively; start with low-hanging fruit. Look for the long times spent adjusting. Work on those areas first. You will learn a lot. Develop good local partners who can machine new fasteners for you. This is where you will get some nice benefit that cannot easily be replicated by your competitors and give you a durable competitive advantage.

The Right Tool

There are precision tools and there are flexible tools. An adjustable wrench is a flexible tool. It is great for the homeowner who doesn't want to own a large quantity of open and close-end wrenches. However, by being adjustable, it requires time for adjustment (slow). If you are serious about Setup Reduction, you need to invest in good quality, precision tools, which can be used immediately and quickly, without adjustment.

When selecting tools, look for tools that can be easily inserted into the fastener without slipping out and without a lot of fumbling around. The tool should have a handle that can be easily and precisely rotated without slipping. When given the choice between a manual tool and an automated tool, consider carefully. In most cases, an automatic tool will work more quickly than a manual tool. But, you must consider keeping the tool charged and whether the tool offers the proper torque and precision necessary for the adjustment.

Color-Code Tools to Fasteners

During your makeready, you want operators to immediately locate the needed tool for a fastener, immediately use the tool with minimal turns, and to put the tool back in its proper place quickly, ready for the next use. Not only does this require thought in where tools are located but you should also consider color-coding screw and bolt heads to wrench color. So, if you have three different head or drive styles used on a binder, make sure you have red, blue, and green heads color-coded so that anyone can grab the right tool the first time. Think of the benefit. Not only will your regular operators become more efficient but also any stand-in operators will be much faster during the makeready. Maintenance crews will work more efficiently. Press helpers can jump in quickly when asked to tighten or loosen a bolt. It simply makes the process much more user-friendly.

FIGURE 3: *Color coding your tools and fasteners can aid in quick identification*

Using color for quick identification is a key aspect to visual management, a primary Lean tenant. The goal of Lean is to make everything visible so that not only does the operator know a task is being done correctly but any observer, regardless of expertise, can know a task is being performed properly. A casual observer can easily see that a blue wrench is used with a blue bolt. It makes everything quick, easy, and efficient. Remember, the goal is to ensure that all non-valued activities are eliminated. And searching for a wrench, even for two seconds is time that when multiplied more than 100 times per year can have accumulating impact.

A thorough analysis of all setup tools and fasteners is very important to improve makeready time. If it is not obvious already, we are looking for both incremental and breakthrough improvements in the process. So, do not skip even the small improvements. Not only will you gain a few seconds on makeready time but also as important, you send the message to the entire team that we are looking at the smallest of details and questioning the most common of practices. Step three involves analyzing and standardizing all setup tools and fasteners. Look closely at your entire process and you will likely find any number of places to improve.

One final note: it will be tempting to simply discount fasteners as "part of the press." It may be true that reengineering fasteners for your press or binder nay not make economic sense (though do get some estimates, please). Nonetheless, it is an important Lean principle to go through the exercise to identify those activities (and fasteners) that result in non-valued time. Go ahead, call the time you spend adjusting them what it is: waste. Go through the activity to identify all fasteners that result in wasted time. By doing so, you will be better situated when you replace equipment in the future. Learning to see waste is half the battle. And it will take lots of reinforcement, as most employees do not naturally think that way. Now, on to step four.

As you think about your current processes, identify some fasteners or tools that are influencing your setup time negatively?

7 Put Tools and Supplies Close By and In an Organized Manner

The fourth step in Setup Reduction is to focus on the placement of tools and supplies. You will want to use the *3 Easies* principle we mentioned earlier in the book. Except, now that we have discussed fasteners, let us make it the *4 Easies*:

- Easy to see

- Easy to get

- *Easy to use*

- Easy to put back

The objective is to have the right tool or supply item within arm's reach of use, whenever possible. The tool or supply should be clearly labeled and easy to identify. Visual management is key in organizing tools and supplies, as the focus is to minimize confusion as to the location, or which tool to select. How many times have you either experienced or witnessed an operator looking for a wrench?

Tool Placement at the Point of Use

Reducing setup time involves having the right tool at the right time. Think about the Pitstop mentality we discussed earlier. How quick would a Pitstop be if the seven individuals involved in racecar maintenance did not have their tire guns or their tire jack? What if they went looking for them at the moment the car pulled in? Instead, these Pit teams spend hours and hours strategizing about tool placement, handling, use, and retrieval. It is their fulltime job. They are very methodical and understand that fractions of a second win races.

Now, picture a typical pressroom. The tools often belong to the operator, not the press or team. So, the operators keep their tools in their toolboxes. Experience suggests that leaving a tool out invites that tool to be borrowed or stolen. The emphasis is on keeping tools from going missing, not on being in the right location for use. The operator makes multiple trips to their toolbox locating each tool as needed and putting back to avoid it going missing. Each operator may have different types of tools. Or they may not have the right tool so they pull out the adjustable wrench.

The model used in Setup Reduction is to focus on taking your new standardized tool set and locating the tools in strategic location(s) and making them visible and accessible. Tool shadow boards are often used because they provide a location for hanging tools, within arm's reach, and also help to remind operators where each tool resides. Operators are trained to put tools back, which is easy to do since they reside within arm's reach of their use.

Shadow boards are certainly not the only option. But they are a good option. Sometimes tools are placed magnetically on equipment, on shelves, or in other appropriate locales.

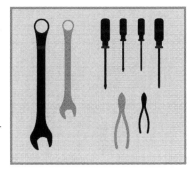

Safety is always a concern in relation to tool placement...and it should be. Never place a tool board where the operator has to reach across an open press unit or hold a wrench over a stitcher pocket. Safety always trumps expediency.

FIGURE 4: *Shadow boards are a great way to organize tools. Missing tools (gray) are apparent.*

Once safety has been considered, the next goal is to have your new standardized, minimized, color-coded tools within arm's reach. To do so may mean you have multiple sets of tools, particularly on large equipment where walking between units is necessary. Why have a single plate wrench that requires operators to walk to retrieve it when you can purchase a second wrench for less than $50? It just makes no sense. Have a plate wrench on a shadow board right next to each unit, within arm's reach of where it is used. Not only will the tool be used more quickly, but also it will be put back in place.

Poorly placed tools are easy to see from your video and spaghetti map. Do you recall all that movement you saw when you focused on your current state? How much motion was expended retrieving tools or supplies? During your analysis, identify where the operator walked after retrieving the tool and that is the location you want to store the tool, where it is easy to see, easy to get, easy to use, and easy to put-back.

"Point of Use Storage" of Consumables

Just as tools are placed in strategic locations, consumables should also be placed at the point of use. The "Easies" principle applies for supplies too. Like tools, be sure to analyze your consumables to ensure you are using the right materials for your operation. It may be that you have three different types of consumables when only two are actually needed. It may be that you can standardize on suppliers so you don't have to keep several iterations of consumables press side. Take the time to first analyze and standardize your consumables. Then, identify the right location for them, at the point of use.

Like tools, consumables should be within arm's reach of where they are used. Shelves and cabinets should be strategically located. Again, look at your current state video and identify where your operator is headed after grabbing the supply item. Then, try to locate your storage as close as is reasonable to that task or operation.

Consumables present a different challenge than tools because they are consumed and therefore must be replenished and disposed. As you work on your Setup Reduction techniques, identify how spent consumables will be disposed. Since disposal is an external setup task, the operator should not be walking spent plates very far during a makeready. They should be placed just one arm's reach away from the print station. A separate task can involve removing the spent material to its final disposal or recycling location.

Now, how do you know how much material to store and how to initiate replenishment? To answer that question, you need to first consider the goals of Setup Reduction and visual management. Visual management is all about reducing visual clutter and improving operator efficiency...all while reducing waste and mistakes. So, you will want to make sure your consumables are placed in an orderly manner, logically placed so as to minimize confusion for the operator. Stacks and stacks of old supplies add confusion and minimize the operator's ability to quickly identify and grab the correct supply. Large quantities of a single consumable make for storage challenges and inventory management issues. But worse is running out of material, such that the operator has to walk to locate new consumables. What is needed is a *Kanban* system.

Kanban for Replenishment

Kanbans are used to signal replenishment. They are a visual signal that more material is needed. When used properly, Kanbans facilitate the reduction of stored material at the point of use. You do not have to retain high consumable inventories press side if you have a reliable Kanban system.

Let us talk for a moment about roll and sheet stock. Most companies use some method to "call" stock to the press. It may simply be the pressroom supervisor telling a warehouse employee to bring out the stock or it may be a visual signal, like a Kanban. It is fairly easy to stay on top of the press' demand with large rolls of paper. When the press is down to one roll in the queue, a fork clamp driver comes out from the stock room with another roll. It is fairly easy to see the need when we are talking about big rolls of paper. This exact same concept can be used for all materials, though the visual queue must be well constructed. . However, when items are small, or used less frequently, or used intermittently, the Kanban system needs to be more intentional.

Only materials that are used daily or weekly should be kept at the work cell. All other materials are brought out with the job, during the premakeready.

The general rule of thumb is to store enough material to be consumed in a shift or less. More than that will only clutter the work area. Your Kanban system will be used to regularly replenish your point of use storage of supplies and consumables.

Let us consider ink now. Assuming they are used regularly, process colors and coatings should probably be kept press side if not pumped. Typically, only two cans or kits should be kept press side. One of the cans will be in use and the other serves as point of use storage, ready to be brought into service when the other can is empty. As this second can is brought into service, this signals replenishment. Exactly how that signal happens can vary, depending on the organization. I would suggest getting a good book on Kanbans to really determine a fail-proof method for signaling replenishment. Many folks simply place a signal on a shelf and cover the signal with the can when in inventory. As the can is removed, it signals the need. However, that assumes someone is walking around looking for signals. Other methods can be used but remember, the goal is to make it visible.

Now what about specialty inks and coatings? They should be prepared and brought out with the job, not stored press side. The premakeready process is used to stage materials, plates, job tickets, and such. Specialty inks should be included as well. And more importantly, the specialty ink should go back with the job when completed, not kept at the press, cluttering the work area. Remember the fifth S of 5s? Sustaining a clean work area is a challenge and should remain an ongoing Lean focus.

Reducing Motion Waste: The Setup Cart

A very popular tool for improving makeready time is the use of a setup cart. A setup cart is a movable workstation used for staging materials (premakeready) and then rolled out press side. But it is more than a wagon. If designed well, it is a complete makeready station that brings all tools and consumables directly press side...within arm's reach of where the makeready occurs. A well-designed setup cart radically improves makeready as all supplies that are not kept at the point of use are brought out on wheels and temporarily placed at the point of use, in a sequentially organized manner, ready for the makeready. Depending on the work area, carts can be very effective.

The best setup carts are those designed by operators, who understand the sequence of their makeready and know how they want materials staged. Most carts require a couple of iterations to get them perfected so do not design a cart and then turn around and build six of them. Build one, use it for a while, and then improve it. After using a cart for a period of time, operators will realize what works well and what needs improving. It may be that insufficient room is available for return inks. Perhaps the plates should be rotated 90 degrees for better transportation. There could be numerous problems but you will not know until you start to use one. Let your operators design one, then build it and use it for a while. Throughout Setup Reduction, you should revisit prior steps to verify improvements have been achieved and to look for better, more efficient methods. For example, after incorporating a setup cart, you may want to video your makeready again to ensure improvement in reducing waste and motion.

Placing of tools and consumables close by and in an organized manner is critical for reducing setup times. Motion will be minimized, while searching for tools or locating stocks and inks will be reduced. Your videos will be essential in your analysis. Then, you will be ready for step five.

As you think about your current processes, where do you see the location of tools influencing your makeready time negatively?

_____

_____

_____

_____

_____

_____

_____

_____

8 Use Positioning and Registration Aids to Speed Setup Time

In order to improve makeready time with your press, binder, or rewinder, you will want to make sure that all installed components and all settings are adjusted correctly the first time. You especially do not want to take a long time adjusting something, which later will need fine-tuning. You want to make sure your macro adjustment is perfect on start-up. Actually, you want to make sure your micro adjustment is perfect on start-up too, but that is not always possible, at least for most equipment.

Registration is a critical part of printing. Registration must be controlled from plate to plate, first down color to substrate, then color-to-color, backside printing, print-to-cut, and finally finishing. There are plenty of places and opportunities for misregistration to occur.

During a makeready, the operator may set the feeder and delivery for a particular substrate. The operator may also mount the plates and focus on registering each color. On a folder, the operator focuses on hitting the fold marks to ensure good crossovers. Frequently, getting registration involves numerous iterations and lots of time setting up and adjusting.

The fifth step in our Setup Reduction processes is to minimize setup time by using positioning and registration aids so that accurate registration occurs on startup with no additional adjustment. The objective here is to "Get it right the first time." In other words, when you make a registration setting, such as setting a buckle folder or positioning a die, get it right the first time. I realize that may sound unrealistic but let me explain.

Identifying Critical Registration Points

Registration is largely a mechanical function. As such, observation can often tell us all we need to know about where registration is critical and where registration fails and frequently requires adjustment. Experienced operators can tell immediately where they struggle with achieving and holding tight registration. In theory, mechanical registration is achievable the first time. If it is achievable the third, fourth, or fifth time, it is achievable the first time. It simply means you need to employ a better system in positioning your initial settings.

With some thought, you can probably identify several key areas where registration can go wrong:

- Imaging plates: plate to plate

- Punching and bending plates

- Mounting plates

- Substrate bounce between units

- Substrate stability between units (tension or moisture)

- Fit (improper packing)

- Skewed plate

- Circumferential, lateral, tangential adjustments

- Substrate to finishing equipment

Certainly this list is not exhaustive, but you get the idea. Your operators and process experts will do a thorough job identifying the problem areas and creating a comprehensive list for your environment. At what points along your process does misregistration occur and frequently need adjusting?

Now, the question is this: are there any possible ways you could use positioning aids, registration aids, or indicators which pinpoint registration accuracy before printing, folding, die cutting, or binding? Are there ways to preregister components? Are there alignment tools that could help to ensure accuracy during setup, so it is not just "close" but actually "correct"?

We are not naive. We understand that some equipment simply isn't capable of holding tight registration, much less facilitating initial registration. Some equipment can hold register when achieved but there is simply no way to use a positioning aid during the setup process. For these reasons, it is easy to dismiss step five. We encourage you not to. We hope you do not conclude you cannot preregister...until you put some brainpower behind it. Now is when you want to bring in some fresh eyes and start asking the hard questions. Get your operators thinking outside their normal work habits.

Using Jigs, Templates, or Marks

Jigs and templates help the operator to accurately set a variable adjustment. We do this already. Sheetfed press operators grab a handful of sheets to position as they set their feeder and delivery guide. The paper serves as a jig (mechanical positioning aid), controlling the position for setting guides and joggers. Where else can this happen? Where else can jigs be used?

Jigs and templates are more logical for standardized or repeat work. It is difficult to have a jig made for every custom job unless there is the possibility of a rerun; it simply does not make economic sense. However, sheet and roll sizes are often repeated. So, why not make jigs for common sheet sizes and roll sizes. They can be used for setting feeders, delivers, roll stands, cutting dies, foil-stamping dies, and rewinds.

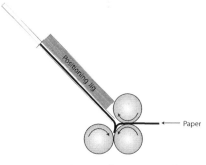

FIGURE 5: *A jig, in this case a wooden stick, can be used to quickly and accurately set redundant or common positions, like on this buckle paper folder.*

Let us revisit the previous list of registration locations and see where mechanical positioning tools can be applied:

- Imaging plates: plate to plate

- Punching and bending plates

- Mounting plates

- Substrate bounce between units

- Substrate stability between units (tension or moisture)

- Fit (improper packing)

- Skewed plate

- Circumferential, lateral, tangential adjustments

- Substrate to finishing equipment

Imaging plates—plate to plate

Depending on your plating system, loading plate media into your imaging device may require precise alignment. A jig or template may be useful for this process. The goal is to ensure that placement is exact for both the physical plate and the image on the plate. It may be that your platesetter handles all that for you. But you also may need to calibrate it periodically to ensure accurate placement of each plate and image. Run a test target to see how repeatable your plate imaging is. Is the plate positioned the same each time? Is the plate imaged in the same location each time? Can a tool help with the loading of plates in your imager? Do you have a standard process for calibrating your machine and checking for position repeatability?

Punching and bending plates

Once you are sure that you are imaging in the same location on each plate, there is subsequent plate processing that can influence mechanical position. Some plates must be cut (flexo), punched, or bent (offset). Each of these steps could lead to imperfect registration on press. Where common sizes occur, there is potential for a jig or template to be used for these processes. Most offset systems use manual or automated punching and bending. Review your procedures and review the repeatability of your punch/bender. You are looking for more precise ways to ensure squareness and position when punching and bending. It is critical that the plates come out with exactly the same position for bends and punched patterns. If not, it is time to revisit the process. Again, calibration and standardization are critical. Again, a jig may help in this process to ensure repeatable positioning.

Mounting plates, Fit (improper packing), and Skewed plates

Flexo converters mount plates offline while most offset printers mount their plates at the press. Either way, there is significant opportunity for imperfect registration as a result of plate mounting. Even with pin mounting system, plates may be thousandths of an inch off on startup. That needs to change. You need to work through the engineering and procedures to make sure those plates are mounted in register, so that plate mounting is removed from the makeready equation. Calibration, standardized processes and positioning aids need to be implemented across press lines and operators.

Some techniques that have improved plate mounting include video systems (flexo), pin systems, and physical stops. Check when clamping plates to see what the registration tolerance is there too. Is there any "slop" in the process of clamping offset plates on press? If so, you have to rectify that variability. Do not over tighten clamps (offset) or apply undue pressure when securing plates to mounting tapes (flexo) as this may skew or stretch the plate. Fit can be a problem with improper plate packing (offset). It is critical that all cylinders are the same diameter and circumference, so be certain to take a scientific look at all components that influence circumference and concentricity.

A well-defined operating procedure for mounting plates may do wonders. A great deal of preregistration can happen simply by using best practices on mounting plates. Modern presses with automated plate mounting systems should be calibrated and tuned periodically. These systems should be repeatable both within and across press units.

Substrate bounce and stability between units

Substrates can bounce or change dimensionally between printing units, impacting registration and fit. Bounce is certainly a frustrating problem as it can often be difficult to determine the exact location. At the speed modern presses are run, it is amazing that we can register inks from unit to unit at all. Jigs and templates may not help here but ensuring that other setup procedures are meticulously followed (remember the pit crew), should help to minimize the occurrence of bounce and fit. A comprehensive maintenance program, like *Total Productive Maintenance* (TPM), will also help ensure minimal bounce and fit issues.

> Total Productive Maintenance is a philosophy that attempts zero breakdown status of equipment. A structured process using preventative and predictive maintenance strategies helps to achieve this goal, important for just-in-time production.

Circumferential, Lateral, Tangential and Finishing Adjustments

Registering your sheet or web going into the first unit is critical. Like all steps in Setup Reduction, you will want to use a standardized process to set side-guides, head stops, or web guides. For common stock or roll sizes, jigs or templates may help in this process as well, especially for manual presses. The goal is to get the substrate position correctly the first try. Use tools to help you do so. Since selecting the correct jig is an external SMED task, make sure that the operator is not selecting the positioning aid while the press is sitting idle. Registration is frequently analyzed through visual means anyway, so use visual tools to position these components correctly the first time.

If on startup the colors are not in register, color-to-color adjustment is usually achieved by moving the plate cylinder. Adjustment may be necessary, and the next chapter is about minimizing adjustment. But what prevents you from ensuring the plates are mounted in such a way that the colors are in register with each other? The press is usually capable of holding circumferential and lateral registration to within common tolerances. So, if the last job is in register, why can't the next job start up in register? Again, ask the question. There may not be a simple answer to that question but I suspect you have some sharp operators and maintenance engineers who may have an answer to that question. And the answer may surprise you and lead to quicker startups.

To be fair, web printing requires roll tension to achieve registration and tension changes with press speed. So, it may be difficult achieving perfect preregistration on startup, but do not be afraid to identify and document every challenge. Equipment manufacturers are regularly looking for engineering solutions to the printer's problems, like stepped tension algorithms based on press speed. But, your job is to analyze, ask the difficult questions, explore all solutions no matter how unique or crazy, document problems, and focus on continuous improvement. Remember, Setup Reduction was developed over years and years, but today it is a world-class methodology.

Narrow-web flexo printers mount their plates off line and then place them in the printing units. Older presses have no indication how the cylinder is to be oriented when placed in the unit. So, how can a jig or template aid in this process. It is too simple to just put a mark on the cylinder because flexo printers use variable size cylinders so unless you standardize cylinder to print unit, you'll need another method.

We worked with one printer to develop a system for imaging a mark on the plate, such that the mark orients how the plate is positioned during installation (assuming ink sequence is known when making plates). That is a simple solution for sure, but it is effective. Now, the operator simply puts the cylinder in with the mark at the 12:00 O'clock position for macro preregistration. It works every time as long as the correct cylinder is placed into the correct printing unit. The prepress operator images the marks in the correct location based on a simple calculation. Preregistration at its best, in this case using a simple mark imaged on the plate.

Gauges: Numerical Settings and Other Measurable Devices

Premakeready and preregistration can also be achieved with the use of gauges. Numerical settings are ideal because they are so repeatable. So, just like one "sights-in" a firearm, gauges can be used to "sight-in" registration. Whenever numerical gauges can be used for registration, the settings are usually repeatable. So, look for opportunities on any of the areas listed above to implement gauges. Is it possible for your lateral or circumferential adjustments to use gauges, if they don't already? Is it possible to engrave a scale onto your cylinders for visual alignment during plate mounting?

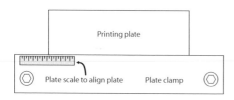

Printing plate

Plate scale to align plate   Plate clamp

Gauges are not only terrific for ensuring correct registration, but they also work well for the next step in the process, which is to minimize adjustment. If your operator knows he needs to move the blue plate 0.008" toward the operator, can your gauges ensure you hit that correctly the first time? Gauges allow for precise movements and repeatable placement.

Where can gauges be used? Well, many modern presses use gauges or PLCs (programmable logic controllers) for many functions on a press or binder. But older presses often do not have sufficient ways to adjust known amounts. So, it is difficult to have repeatability.

Try this: send your operator away for a moment. Then move registration on a color by 0.012" circumferentially and 0.07" laterally. Oh, go ahead and skew the plate while you are at it. Can your operator bring it back in register in one try? Or will it take iterations? A move...then another move...etc?

Gauges are the tools that can help quantify these registration adjustments. Gauges are measurement tools. So, using a gauge for any registration adjustment allows it to be precise and repeatable. Look for ways to add gauges to your processes. Some situations may be simpler than you think. If it is not feasible to add gauges to your equipment, be sure to document the desire, so you are better prepared when you are analyzing new equipment.

Making it Visual

Finally, make registration visible. Make everything about registration visible. Make it obvious when things are not in register. This means having *obvious* and *informative* marks. If your product will not allow that, fine, make them tiny. But, make sure you have marks throughout the workflow that can be used to ensure you have all registration points accounted for and can immediately see a problem. The faster misregistration is identified, the faster it is corrected.

Make your standardized premakeready and makeready procedures visible. Make the selection of the jig an external task—part of the premakeready. Make any jigs or templates well labeled or colored so they are used at the right time and in the right manner. If you have a manual press, you may want to color code all circumferential knobs blue and lateral knobs green. Or you may want chose to use a color system on your marks and your knobs so you can simply say "move 0.004" to red (where red references toward the operator side and is colored as such on the press console). The goal is to simplify and make things very visible so all individuals can see what is happening, what needs to be done, and how to rectify the problem quickly.

What about Automation?

We have been speaking so much about older equipment; it certainly makes sense to discuss the use of JDF and CIP4 before concluding this chapter. Where do these technologies fit in with Setup Reduction? Right in the middle, of course. The whole purpose of CIP4 is to automate the setting of equipment so that adjustments are minimized: "lights out printing." Said differently, the focus is on "getting it right the first time." So CIP4 totally makes sense for improving makeready.

However, in many situations, you will need to invest a substantial amount of money to implement a JDF workflow. We would prefer that you initially focus on "people" solutions, rather than technology solutions...at least at first. It is easy to discount many of the principles discussed in this book and instead "buy" your Setup Reduction solution. The problem with that approach is that others can replicate your competitive advantage fairly easy. In fact, it is not an advantage...it is a way to stay current. You may buy six months of advantage but others will catch up when you simply buy commercially available products. Your advantage comes from your processes, not your equipment—unless of course you are making your equipment and retaining all rights to its use.

Technology absolutely will help you in reducing makeready times. But, you can still remove much time in the makeready process by working on using manual registration aids. As easy as it is to "buy" Setup Reduction with technology, it is just as easy to discount these principles and say you cannot afford Setup Reduction. You absolutely can. It is about your people, not your pocket book. Once you have mastered the people principles of Setup Reduction, then you can focus on technology. When you have accomplished using registration aids, then you will be ready for step six, working to eliminate adjustment.

As you think about your current processes, where do you see the ability to use positioning aids during your makeready?

9 Work to Minimize Adjustment

Makeready involves adjustments. It is exactly what we do during the makeready. We get the plates and inks in the press, we set up the feeder and delivery, and we print. Then we start adjusting: usually registration first, then matching color targets, then fine-tuning everything and eliminating any defects that may result from starting and stopping the press so often. How much time and materials are wasted doing all this adjustment? A lot, I am sure you will agree.

Step six in our Setup Reduction process is to eliminate adjustment time. Steps five and six actually go hand-in-hand and support each other. We use positioning aids and templates to speed initial settings, but they also minimize adjustment time. If we can hit the target on the initial setup, no adjustment is necessary. But if we do not hit the target the first time, we focus on measured adjustments so that when we do need to make a move, we hit the target the first adjustment. The goal is to make a single adjustment for each parameter, at most. We want to build in process steps to make sure we don't have to "nudge" our way to the right target. Once we realize a move is needed, how can we hit that adjustment the first time, in a single, precise move?

Premakeready to Reduce Adjustment

Let us start with the simple premise that our two primary areas of concern on a press makeready are registration and color. We wrote at length in the last chapter about using positioning aids to achieve registration. We focused on using jigs and templates to ensure we get guides, stops, brushes, and other components to the right settings to begin with. We also wrote about the benefit of using numerical gauges, so that if adjustment is needed, you can make the necessary move and hit the target correctly the first time. We will spend more time on adjustment in this chapter but put our focus more on color matching rather than registration.

In packaging, spot colors are used extensively for matching brand colors. Unfortunately, far too much press time is devoted to adjusting the ink to match the initial ink drawdown. This is particularly true in flexo and gravure printing, where extenders and colorants are added to the fluid inks right on press. The ink is toned or extended, and a print is made. The press is stopped and the color evaluated, at which time more adjustments takes place. Why can't all color adjustments be done as a premakeready function?

There are many good off-press ink-proofing tools available today that can mimic press conditions quite well. These tools have comparable anilox rolls or ink metering systems (flexo) to presses. They can match press conditions very well, with the exception of press speed. But even then, it may be possible to compensate for press speed by reducing anilox cell volume slightly, in a predictable way. The point is, the press should not be used as an ink adjustment tool but rather as a manufacturing tool. Take ink color matching off press. And when adjustments are needed, use a strategy that will allow you to make your adjustment in one shot. Make sure you measure your ink on a scale so you know the ratios of color base you are adding. Document the process so that you can begin to understand the influence of specific amounts of ink components? Make the process repeatable so that the next time the color is run, you can begin from an accurate or closer starting point.

Process colors also require adjustment on press. In most cases, the ink itself is not modified press side but the ink keys (offset) or metering system requires adjustment. Like spot inks, careful attention to the printing system can substantially reduce adjustment iterations. This requires some understanding of color and the use of new tools for achieving gray tones. It is well understood that color is most pleasing when gray balance is achieved in photographic imagery. When grays are neutral, colors generally fall into place. And with a good substrate and clean inks, a pleasing color gamut is achievable quickly with balanced CMY grays.

Near-neutral calibration or G7® will help any press achieve pleasing gray overprints much faster, and that means less makeready time. This requires that your ink sets have standardized hue angles (ISO 2846/12647) and that your cutback (neutral density) curves are calibrated to achieve a neutral three-color overprint. During press startup, color is achieved much more quickly with much less adjusting. In fact, many printers who run near-neutral calibration do very little ink key adjusting (offset) or ink modification (flexo). Color is achieved very quickly and adjustments are minimized. By doing one's homework and using the right ink set with the correct curves, less color correcting on press is needed. Prepress supports the value creating function and helps the pressroom achieve sellable products more quickly.

Premakeready means having a controlled prepress workflow. For that matter, premakeready means good design and photography. When images are good to begin with, and a good workflow is applied, high-quality plates come to the pressroom, with the correct curves applied so that the press is not asked to compensate for poor imagery or plate production. The press is a manufacturing process not an artist's canvas.

Ink Presets

Modern presses often have the ability to digitally scan a plate or file to preset ink fountain keys accordingly (offset). This certainly can speed up changeover times. When available, the pressroom should take advantage of such systems to reduce makeready time.

The Role of Maintenance in Setup Reduction

Total Productive Maintenance (TPM) is a detailed Lean topic beyond the scope of this text. However, a comprehensive maintenance program is vital for Setup Reduction. In offset printing, where more than twenty-five rollers make up typical ink and dampening systems, well-tuned systems make the makeready process responsive. If you are looking for quick color responses, you need a print unit that is well tuned in terms of level, tram and pressure. When ink keys are actuated on the press console, we need a rapid response. We need minimum fountain solution and minimum fountain roll sweep. The point is that a well-maintained press will respond quickly to the press operator's actions. A press in poor condition will not. Maintenance can play a significant role in rapid equipment response, allowing the press and bindery to do their job in increasing value creation.

> Line, level, and tram represent the three-dimensional space in which presses are erected and aligned for optimum production. Each roller or cylinder must be positioned in parallel with other rolls in a 3D space. In a rectangle, think of Line as the length, level as the width, and tram as the height.

Measured Adjustments: Focus on Numerical Measures and Tolerances

As noted in the previous chapter, numerical controls are important to ensure measured movements during adjustment. Whenever possible, you want to use *measured adjustments*. The term "measured adjustment" means scaled and precise. This means that whatever adjustment you make should be achievable with a single scaled move. Further, measured adjustments make repeating a job much quicker.

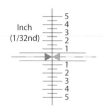

FIGURE 6: *RTT Registration Target. Arrows point to a ruled target for scaled registration*

We advise you take a structured approach to using measured adjustments. Let us look at some makeready adjustments on a flexo print station and how you might modify your process to include measured adjustment:

- Doctor blade pressure: is it possible to put a scale or pressure gauges on the connection/pressure screws?

- Print cylinder position: is it possible to correlate lateral and circumferential adjusting knobs (clicks) to distance (scaled)?

- Plate cylinder impression: is it possible to use pressure gauges on your impression settings to measure the amount of pressure to increase?

- Ink: is it possible to incorporate a simple thermometer or pH meter to monitor ink in the fountain to monitor ink health during a run?

Of course, it is always better to engineer measured controls into the press during the design phase. But some retrofits may be achievable with little expense and creative thought. And, do not discount manual measurements. While it is true you do not want to expend time measuring during a makeready, if a single measurement can result in a single adjustment, the net gain may justify the measurement. But it all starts with making your adjustments scaled.

Make it Visible and Informative

We spoke in the last chapter about making each variable visible, such that out of specification production can immediately be seen. This not only applies when you use positioning aids but also in making adjustments. Scaled adjustments are best because the measurement can correlate directly with a control component. When that is impossible or difficult, visual control targets can offer single-adjustment feedback; they are informative, providing the operator the necessary information to make a single adjustment.

Control targets are used in printing and finishing all the time. However, many of them do not provide obvious information related to the out-of-compliance production and how to correct the defect. Few of them provide the operator specific information for making a single adjustment. Lean suggests that the control targets should be easily seen with clear direction for how to correct the defect, so that anyone looking at the sheet can know what to do.

There are a number of examples of commonly used control targets. Each serves a specific purpose—to indicate when a variable or attribute is out of tolerance. However, some are not particularly visible or don't provide clear indication of the correction. Below, you will find a variety of "ideas" to make marks more visible and informative. First, you will see that typical mark followed by a more visible version.

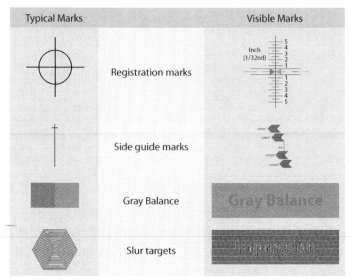

Typical Marks		Visible Marks
	Registration marks	
	Side guide marks	
	Gray Balance	
	Slur targets	

Document to Manage Future Knowledge

The 10-step Setup Reduction Process for Print Manufacturing:

1. Benchmark your current makeready
2. Minimize Internal processes
3. Analyze, minimize, and standardize all setup tools and fasteners
4. Put tools and supplies close by and in an organized manner
5. Use positioning and registration aids to speed setup time
6. Work to minimize adjustment
7. Use parallel setup processes
8. Standardize, coordinate & improve your makeready
9. Mistake proof the process
10. When all else fails, reengineer the process

Finding improvements in steps five and six can be challenging. Some printers simply do not work hard in these areas because they just do not see where improvements can be made. They give up. I agree, these are two of the more difficult areas to find big gains. Adjustment strategies can save much time, but it takes empowered employees to discover the relationships between variables. Setup time can decrease as your organization gains process and system expertise. But even when an operator develops a unique strategy, knowledge is difficult to manage and transfer across an organization. If one press operator has determined the precise amount of pH adjuster needed to raise 0.5 pH units for a particular ink, how can that knowledge be transferred across your entire pressroom?

There are a number of approaches for transferring knowledge across an organization. Blogs, memos, wikis, training meetings, standard operating procedures, and informal discussions are all approaches. Whatever your organization decides, you need to make sure you have one or more individuals in charge of documenting what you learn.

Documentation is critical. It is the first step in managing knowledge. Once you document what operators learn about processes, they can be confirmed and then deployed and standardized. Only when adjustment strategies are institutionalized will you see gains made from your efforts in step six, minimizing adjustment.

As you think about your current makereadies, how can you minimize time spent adjusting variables like register and color?

10   Use Parallel Setup Processes

Step seven in our Setup Reduction process is to use parallel setup activities. Consider this: popular racing pit crews use a jackman and two tire changers for changing tires. Why do tire men only change two tires during a pitstop instead of four? Is it because they cannot change four? Or is it because it is more efficient to use two individuals working in parallel? Why do they use someone to focus solely on the jack? The answers are probably obvious; they can achieve faster results by using parallel processing. They have faster changeovers when two or more people work in tandem. This same principle is useful during a press or finishing makeready.

Most companies today hire a lead operator and depending on the size of the press, a variety of helpers. But each operator generally has well-defined duties. One or two may focus on feeding pockets or loading rolls or sheets. Another focuses on the delivery. Still another emphasizes checking press sheets and making register and color adjustments. During a makeready, their duties also change to focus on setup. Interestingly though, their job descriptions, duties and the majority of their performance review criteria are often focused more on the press run, than the makeready. Makeready is a secondary function for many companies, not the operator's primary function. Think of this in particular when you offer performance appraisal feedback. What is the ratio of time, or comments, you spend on operators running the equipment versus setting it up?

Very few companies recognize the importance of using additional personnel during makeready. In nearly all cases, the cost of additional labor is far less than the hourly rate of a production press. Why not shave your makeready time by 10-30% simply by putting additional trained personnel on the changeover process? Can you imagine if the driver of a racecar had to jump out and change the tires, fill the gas tank, clean the window, and so forth? It sounds absurd but why do we expect our operators to do that very thing without additional support? The answer gets back to our view of makeready as a chargeable item. Simply because customers are accustomed to paying a makeready charge does not mean it is valued.

This also gets unconsciously reinforced with our understanding of roles and duties. Once we formally establish a crew for a given piece of equipment we tend to focus on the crew's total ownership and responsibilities for preparing and running the equipment. Our real focus should be on optimizing the business in creating value and eliminating waste but we sometimes let other concepts, like our crew definition get in the way. It may be time to change our understanding about how we perform a makeready.

The Case for Another Helper

The standard argument against additional setup personnel usually focuses around the increased labor cost. If you think about it, even if your job cost goes up by $40 because of an hour of additional labor, reducing twenty minutes of press time nearly always results in an overall decrease in job cost. But there are often strategic ways of realigning your workforce so that individuals have new or different duties, without increasing your payroll. You may be able to deploy one or two individuals who work across your entire pressroom.

One of the best strategies I have seen involves appointing one or two individuals as setup specialists. This individual focuses on staging materials (premakeready), delivering carts press-side, and then working in parallel with other operators to expedite the makeready. The makeready specialist works across multiple press-lines. Of course, this strategy takes substantial coordination, which is part of the learning process and necessary for effective Setup Reduction.

Another strategy is to use 2nd operators as setup specialists. In many cases smaller presses are staffed with two operators, though only one may be needed to monitor the press during a smooth run. It may be possible for that 2nd operator to leave when the press is running well and focus on a makeready somewhere else in the pressroom. Cross training operators adds flexibility to your pressroom or bindery.

Ink technicians may be able to serve specific duties during a press makeready. Again, coordination is critical, as you do not want other presses to go idle while waiting for ink (the neglect of a distracted ink technician). The point is not to get hung up on all the potential pitfalls, but rather to work through the challenges by using your people—empowering them and cross-training them to look differently and to take action to improve.

The same approach can be applied to binders or other finishing equipment. Once a machine is set up well, your setup expert need not stay around to watch the binder run. This individual is free to work on another binder makeready. Conversely, think about how you can engage your entire crew in the setup process by delineating the tasks and determining which tasks can safely be performed in parallel. Perhaps all your pocket feeders can become setup experts. Various approaches can be used to staff additional setup personnel to employ parallel processing.

What Can Be Done in Parallel?

In the first step of our Setup Reduction process, you were asked to bench-mark your current makeready, your "current state." We do this so that we have a basis for measuring improvement. But, we also use that information specifically to focus efforts on each parts of your setup. Let us review quickly what your activity log contains.

The activity log you used for documenting all setup activities included two broad sections: 1) current state documentation; 2) future state analysis. In both sections, part of the documentation includes a place to indicate if the activity is done in parallel with another activity. When you video your makeready, did you see any activities being done simultaneous to other activities? If you have two operators, I sure hope so!

When you look for areas to improve, you want to try to identify some specific situations where an activity could be done in parallel with another task. There are often two situations when this can occur: 1) when redundant activities are being done by the same individual; 2) when any activity does not require a prerequisite activity.

Redundant Makeready Activities

There are many setup activities in the typical printing plant that are redundant. These include each unit on a multicolor press (including mounting plates, cleaning blankets, loading ink, etc.), each pocket on a pocket binder, each buckle section on a buckle folder, each dryer on a flexo or gravure press, and cleaning up printing units. There are probably hundreds of examples just like this if you break them down into discrete tasks. The question is, can the setup of these individual items be done in parallel? Can the work be done safely in parallel? Can time be reduced if done in parallel?

In many cases, the answer is yes; they can be performed in parallel. Presses with servo motors may allow each unit to be driven independently on the press or binder, and subsequently, no additional safety risk is incurred by having multiple operators set up a station. But even with conventional shafted equipment, it may be possible to do some functions in parallel, without compromising safety. It simply takes training, planning, and coordination.

Does it make sense to have six people setting up six printing stations? Probably not. After all, we do not see four individual tire men in a pit crew. Why not? Besides the fact that the racing league limits the number, I suspect the rationale focuses on lack of returns, relative to the safety and efficiency of the operation. Simply put, four people are not twice as efficient as two people and subsequently may create more chaos and injuries. The same may be true on a press or converting operation. You will simply need to test it for yourself. What the magic number of parallel operations is will depend on your environment. However, I can almost assure you that magic number improves with more than one person trained in setup processes and with employees working together.

It is always a bit dangerous making lists in a book like this because you may well know first hand one or more examples will not work in your environment. So be it...you need to make your own list. But, included on your list could be a number of redundant activities, including:

- Mounting plates

- Cleaning blankets

- Loading ink

- Zeroing ink keys

- Swapping anilox rolls out (flexo)

- Cleaning press units

- Installing print cylinders (flexo)

- Draining ink

- Setting impression

- Setting dampening system

- Preinking ink train

- And the list can go on, and on, and on

Activities without Prerequisite Tasks

For the most part, activities in a makeready generally fall into two classes: 1) Those that require a prerequisite task, and; 2) Those that don't require a prerequisite task. Any task that does not rely on something else to be done first is a logical choice for establishing a parallel setup process, since it can be done at any time.

There are many things that do not require a prerequisite. Further, there are many situations where items sit for a period even after the prerequisite task is completed. These also can be done in parallel, at that point.

Here is a sample list of items that may fall into the category of tasks not requiring prerequisite tasks. Again, these may not fit perfectly in your plant and your workflow, but do not be lured into discounting the concept, even though the application is not perfect:

- Setting up the delivery

- Installing dies

- Loading paper

- Acquiring pallets

- Setting up folders or rewinders

- Acquiring rewind cores

If you are struggling to think of items that fit this category, here is a simple solution. Go back to your activity log you did during your benchmarking phase, and for each makeready task, list the prerequisites required before completing that task. If you can list a prerequisite, then you know that the task may not be a good candidate for parallel processing. Anything that you cannot list a prerequisite for is probably perfect for parallel processing… one operator works on it while another operator or setup specialist works on another task.

A Closer Look at Costs

To illustrate this point better, let us look at an actual cost scenario. Using the National Association of Printing Leadership's (NAPL's) CS InterACT-SF 3.0 for calculating hourly cost rates, they show a Heidelberg CD-74-4-P 4-color 29" sheetfed press at an all-inclusive rate right around $200 per hour (75%

productivity), for a two-shift operation. That means, every 15 minutes of press time costs $50 and every minute costs $3.34. If you pay an additional helper $40 per hour (including all benefits), that equates to $10 per 15 minute chunk or $0.67 per minute. Do the economics make sense? Of course, assuming you can use their time wisely and actually cut makeready time.

Some may argue, "It sounds good on paper but let's see it in practice." Significant planning must be in place to ensure that any additional labor is actively making a difference on press or finishing setups. That means they must have well-defined duties, must work in parallel with other operators to reduce the time spent on a particular makeready, and be actively involved in premakeready activities. If you are employing someone at $40 per hour (all inclusive) and that individual is not impacting equipment setup time on an hourly basis, then it may in fact be a net increase in cost. But, with some strategizing, in most cases such a situation makes financial sense.

Where this really makes sense is when you cross-train existing employees to increase your plant's flexibility in moving people around to focus on reducing setup time and costs. Nobody has a plant full of employees who are all 100% productive. Management, and the employees, all know this. Find ways to better utilize existing employees in this process. You will achieve your waste reduction goals and your employees will feel empowered to help make a positive difference in the business. An additional benefit you receive is the more you involve existing employees the more ideas they will have about ways to improve the process.

Remember, It Is About Customer Value

The previous section focuses on the cost justification for hiring one or more employees to focus on parallel processing of makereadies and performing premakereadies—a setup specialist. As noted, it often makes a lot of financial sense to hire such an individual. It may not matter if it makes financial sense initially. Because your motivation for reducing setup times is about increasing customer value. Even if that costs you money, there is a strong case to proceed because in the long-term you will likely decrease makereadies and in the interim you will be building significant customer loyalty.

Go back and review the first chapters of this text. If you do, you will remember that customer value is defined as those items a customer is delighted to pay for. Rarely, if ever, does makeready fall into that category. So, if you want to increase customer value, you will need to reduce your makeready time. If you do not increase customer value, your customers will go somewhere else. And trust me; your competitors are highly focused on this topic. They are reducing makeready time, whether you are or not.

Parallel setup procedures are a great way to reduce specific portions of a makeready substantially. This section alone may reduce your time by 20-30%, depending on the nature of your makereadies. Any redundant activities are a potential for parallel operations. And even non-redundant activities may be appropriate to occur simultaneously with other activities. What it takes are "fresh eyes." As mentioned many times, you need to ask the hard questions and consider alternative views about how makereadies are done. You may find some tremendous timesavings here. You will get even greater results when you standardize, coordinate & improve your makereadies.

Ignoring the cost equation for the moment, where does working in parallel make sense from the standpoint of reducing setup times in your current processes?

_____

_____

_____

_____

_____

_____

_____

11 Standardize, Coordinate & Improve Your Makeready

Up to this point, we have discussed many individual efforts to improve makeready times. Now it is time to really institutionalize what you have achieved. And that is done through standardizing, coordinating, and improving your efforts. This is step eight in the process.

> Institutionalize: to establish (something, typically a practice or activity) as a convention or norm in an organization or culture. Source: Google

Standardize

Throughout this book, we have focused on individual steps. Let us take a moment and review the first seven steps:

1. Benchmark your current makeready
2. Minimize Internal processes
3. Analyze, minimize, and standardize all setup tools and fasteners
4. Put tools and supplies close by and in an organized manner
5. Use positioning and registration aids to speed setup time
6. Work to minimize adjustment
7. Use parallel setup processes

In order to institutionalize your improvements, you will need to put substantial focus on standardizing your processes. You will need to be intentional about this. It will not happen on its own. In contrast, standardization does not happen easily in American business; individualism is a positive character trait for our culture. Thus, you will need to be deliberate and demanding of standardized work practices. This is as true for makereadies as it is for any part of your manufacturing business. Your output should be the same regardless of the operator and your makeready should be the same regardless of the operator.

The rationale is quite simple. Standardization enables:

- Predictable results

- Repeatable results

- A basis for improvement

Did you catch that last bullet? Remember the phrase we used earlier, "You cannot improve a process until you standardize a process." That is a profound understanding. Many think that standardization stifles creativity and hinders best practices. However, when approached correctly, standardization actually enables the integration of best practices throughout a business. It is not about hindering improvement; it is about institutionalizing improvement.

So, what do we standardize? *The entire makeready process.* One of the most effective ways to do this (and it is not easy, by the way), is to process map each task in the makeready. Get your process experts together and let them work through their best methods for setup. It is a difficult process so some coaching may be necessary depending on the egos involved. But it is a necessary process. It simply will not work having "mavericks" in your pressroom doing things as they please. You are looking for the best team, not the best individuals, just like the pit crew.

Once you have process mapped your makereadies (think of this as writing the script for your next benchmarking video), you will want to share this widely throughout your company, coordinating your efforts across press and bindery crews. Allow people to work through their anxieties and let others challenge the best practice? In the end, the team determines the best practice. And everyone agrees to adapt to the new standard...until the team recognizes a better practice.

Coordinate

Coordinating your Setup Reduction procedures sounds simple, but like any initiative that will impact day-to-day production, it can be daunting to get the attention of operators. Of course, if you own your business, the task is a little easier. If you do not, you must get the buy-in of your senior management. Like each step in this process, it takes time. But the rewards will come.

As part of your coordination, you will want to develop standard operating procedures (SOPs). But it cannot stop there. We have seen many companies who develop SOPs only to see them get filed away and out of sight two months later. Standardized work procedures must become part of your culture for you to gain success. This means training, reviewing, assessing, and using performance reviews to reinforce the significance of standardized work. It also means making standard work instructions visible so anyone walking by can tell if a job is being done correctly or not.

But, even more significant than developing SOPs is the actual coordination of real makereadies. In other words, rehearsing.

Did you know you can go to a pit school? Performance Instruction & Training (PIT) in Mooresville, NC offers *PIT Crew U,* a school for learning how to perform in a pit crew. They teach you everything you need to know to be employed on a pit crew in motorsports. They teach, they train, they do stamina exercises, and then they rehearse. Yes, they actually rehearse how to work a jack, change tires, fill the tank, and clean the windshield. But I already know how to do those things. Why should I have to rehearse? If you want to do it at the elite level, you need to know how to do it correctly and in coordination with others. The same is true with a makeready. You know how to do it, but if you want to do it at the elite level in coordination with other professionals, you need to rehearse.

When was the last time you went to a dress rehearsal for a press makeready? Does that make you chuckle? It shouldn't. In reality, your press team needs to have this conversation and actually do a couple of dry runs, or more. Someone needs to document the different duties and the timing of those tasks. The various players need to be identified and trained. Someone needs to write the script and someone needs to direct the effort and lead. Serious improvement takes serious effort and commitment.

Coordination needs to be an ongoing activity, too. This probably means there needs to periodically be an outside set of eyes to offer feedback to the individuals involved. At PIT, they do lots of videotaping during their pit stop training and rehearsing. Then, they review the video as a group to discuss how each activity went. That may be difficult for hour-long makereadies. But when your makereadies start taking 10-15 minutes, periodic reviewing may be in order. Either way, an outside set of eyes is helpful in the coordination of activities during setup.

Communication is always a challenge in a printing plant. Rarely do operators even get a chance to sit down and talk, much less discuss ways to improve a makeready. But that is your challenge. If you want to succeed in Setup Reduction, you will need to make time for communication to occur. Meetings are a good solution but other avenues may be more beneficial. Communication needs to be an integral part of your new culture as you develop better changeover procedures.

Improve

If you are serious about Setup Reduction, you will achieve significant gains by working through this process with your staff. However, you will want to emphasize that this is always about improving. So, no approach to makeready is sacred. Every idea is welcome and every strategy is fair game for improvement. Even after you institutionalize a process, it is still up for improvement. The best approach looks something like this:

1. Develop a makeready solution: putting a shadow board by the binder, for example

2. Standardize it: do similar boards at other binders

3. Look for improvement ideas: revisit the boards and ask for suggestions

4. Test those ideas: have some process experts review the ideas and then test pilot at a station

5. Prove the concept: ensure ideas are indeed an improvement

6. Deploy improvement: deploy throughout the plant if it is an improvement over the original design

This structure is very similar to the Plan, Do, Check, Act (PDCA or PDStudyA) cycle. Then you start the cycle over again, continuously improving as you grow.

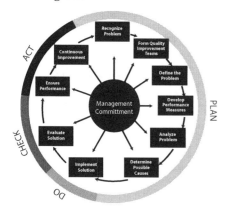

Continuous improvement is a staple for Lean and should be the mantra for every organization. Particularly when it comes to Setup Reduction, you will never have the perfect approach. You simply need to keep improving the process. Sometimes you will take a step backwards before you make a leap forward. The key is to always be looking for improvement.

The printing industry has a rich history. There are many benefits to that and being associated with the industry certainly engenders pride among us. But, the bad side to history is an unwillingness to change and do things differently. For that reason alone, you want to build a culture of improvement and change. The more your employees believe your company accepts and promotes improvements, the more likely you will get where you want to go. Improvement is the foundation for growing your organization.

What specifically are we suggesting you improve? That depends. The best companies develop a culture of improvement and a culture of soliciting suggestions. The improvement process never stops. It is ongoing. You may choose to revisit any of the initial seven steps at anytime. So, if you do not feel that you have made substantial gains in putting tools and supplies close by, revisit that step.

Many companies choose to revisit the entire process periodically in a particularly work area. This is important in building the culture of improvement you desire and in not letting old habits creep back into the setup process. They often want to re-video a makeready to recognize the gains made but to also establish a new benchmark. This now is the basis for the next set of improvements. Or, there may be new equipment or retrofits that allow an activity to change from an internal to an external process. As new tools and fasteners become available, those are natural places to improve. There really is no limit to how and where improvements can be made.

Step eight is to standardize, coordinate, and improve your makeready. This is where the gains are institutionalized. Here is where we go from a couple of "hotshots" to a workforce who understands Setup Reduction. Prior to this step, everything is a "trial." Everything is still just a bunch of brainstorming attempts. But we need to get these improvements integrated into our business and part of our regular practices. We need to get everyone on the same page. We need to get a system in place to facilitate improvements and take them across the plant. Step eight is your place to do just that.

After reading this chapter, how do you see standardization, coordination, and continuous improvement reducing your makeready times?

_____

_____

_____

_____

_____

_____

_____

_____

_____

12 Mistake-Proof the Process

A key principle to Lean thinking is to try to make it very difficult for mistakes to happen and to make it very visible when mistakes do happen. People are prone to having mental lapses and processes are imperfect and have variation. It is a fact. Lean practitioners recognize this aspect of manufacturing and strive for processes and tools that help to eliminate, reduce, or make errors visible when mistakes occur. This principle is referred to as Poka Yoke. It is the ninth step of the Setup Reduction process.

Poka Yoke is an integral part of the continuous improvement principle of Lean. It is not making things "fool-proof" which would neglect the *respect for people* principle. Rather, it recognizes that there is always room for improvement and encourages employees to continually find ways to make it more difficult to produce a defect and pass it on in the manufacturing cycle. Like other aspects of Lean, Poka Yoke brings problems to the surface so they can be resolved and not repeated. This is culturally different than how most of us have been raised, where problems are something to avoid or brush past in an effort to reach an end goal. In Lean, the end goal is achieved by making individual process steps better; Poka Yoke helps you improve your processes by reducing errors during your makeready.

Poka Yoke

Poka Yoke is a Japanese phrase that can be translated as "mistake proof" or "fail safe". The goal of Poka Yoke is to try to make manufacturing processes that simply cannot be completed with mistakes. It focuses on identifying the common sources of mistakes and puts systems in place that eliminate those errors—or, at the least, make the errors visible so that corrective action can be immediately applied before substantial damage is done.

There are many examples of Poka Yoke used in all forms of manufacturing. Some examples of Poka Yoke have been used for years, mostly by integrating sensors in equipment. One example is a double-sheet detector on a sheetfed press or caliper detector on a binder. In both cases, when an inaccurate form comes through (double sheets or double signature), the bad product is ejected or the equipment shuts down. This is a clear example where a mistake is identified and avoided so that the customer does not get a bad book.

Another example is a web break detector and severer. Web break detectors identify when a substrate roll has been broken and immediately shuts down the press to prevent wraps in the cylinders. For high-speed presses, severers are added to cut the web directly in front of a printing unit, reducing inertia's impact on the amount of paper wrapped in the press.

Both of these examples are probably best identified as *sensors*. These are fine examples but they really do not prevent problems, they simply prevent a problem from getting to the customer or creating further downtime. The ultimate goal is to prevent the problem in the first place—to error proof the process. While Poka Yoke is a relatively simple concept, it is indeed difficult to devise tools to truly error-proof processes. Let me propose a few ideas, and then you will need to get your operators thinking about the concept to see what they can come up with. In this chapter, we will focus primarily on Poka Yoke during an equipment makeready.

If you have made it this far into the book, you know our goal is to identify wasteful processes during setup and focus energies on reducing those activities. And, what is more wasteful than making mistakes? Poke Yoke helps to minimize those mistakes during makeready.

Before we jump into discussing Poka Yoke makeready solutions, let us first define "mistake". In the context of this discussion, a mistake can mean an actual defect requiring rework, the creation of a situation where a defect could be produced, or a scenario where additional adjustment is required before good product can be saved. So where do mistakes occur during a makeready? That is a question best answered by employees in your company, using your equipment and your procedures. You need to take the time to work through this discussion with your team and identify where those mistakes occur so that you have a baseline from which to start your focus.

Poka Yoke Examples In Printing And Packaging from *Lean Printing: Pathway to Success (2007 PIA/GATF Press)*

Adding a positioning pin to symmetrical parts making it obvious if they are turned incorrectly.

Notching a printing plate to ensure proper plate positioning.

Web break detectors, web wrap detectors, web severers, and web catchers are all forms of poka-yoke. In the case of a web break detector, when the web is not detected (i.e., when it breaks), the press shuts down before excessive web wrapping at the printing unit occurs.

In one company, operators occasionally inadvertently left a tool in the draft shaft for manually advancing the press, creating a serious safety hazard upon startup when the tool would become airborne. The press was rewired so that the tool had to be in the correct storage location for startup. The tool completed the circuit so the press would only run when the tool was in its proper storage location.

Safety guards are a form of poka-yoke. When the safety guard is raised, the press is de-energized, preventing it from starting.

End-of-roll shut-off detectors prevent the press from running a roll to the core.

Double-sheet detectors prevent unprinted sheets from making it into the delivery and potential blanket damage.

Collating marks or barcoding used on a saddle-stitcher or perfect binder help to ensure all signatures are included in all books. This helps to ensure the binder operator loads signatures in the correct pockets. Stitchers also have calipers for books that have too many or too few signatures in the book.

Poka Yoke Used to Minimize Adjustment

Let us first look at last part of this definition, "additional adjustment required before saving". Much of what we have talked about in this book has focused on strategies to minimize adjustment—or at least doing the brainstorming with your team to minimize adjustment. Poka Yoke ensures that those procedures agreed upon are in place to improve initial registration and improve initial color settings. Poka Yoke helps to prevent or quickly expose when those steps are being skipped or misapplied.

We have discussed various techniques for improving initial register settings, including using jigs and templates for setting up mechanical stops and guides. Poka Yoke takes that process to the next level by ensuring that the register setting cannot be done incorrectly, or makes incorrect positioning immediately visible.

Hopefully you have spent ample time with your process experts identifying each setup activity where registration or color adjustments frequently happen. If you have completed steps one through eight, I know you have had those discussions. Hopefully, you have strategized ways to reduce the need for adjustment. In other words, you have positioned each mechanical guide or stop correctly, mounted plates and cylinders in register, and established your initial settings correctly the first time. Perhaps that means a mechanical jig for setting up deliveries or using pins, or a video scope, or other positioning aid when mounting plates. Perhaps it means re-zeroing your ink keys at the end of a run.

The next step is to make the process mistake-proof. Let me give you a few examples of how this could be done today and then you will hopefully be inspired to raise similar discussions with your employees so that you can effectively Poka Yoke your makeready. Poka Yoking a process is not easy so you will want to train your employees on the principle and then let them work on strategies over a period of time.

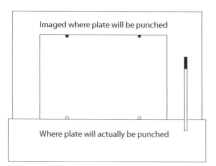

FIGURE 7: *One Poka Yoke method for placement of the printing plate; punching should remove the imaged notches.*

A simple example of Poka Yoke used during makeready is ensuring that your plates can be mounted in only one way. For offset presses, that is easily achieved by notching, punching, or bending plates. They can then only be mounting in one orientation, assuming punching and bending has been achieved correctly. However, if not punched or bent correctly, plates can easily be installed upside down. So, can you think of a Poka Yoke method for ensuring that plates are placed in a punch/bender properly? Are there ways to image or notch a plate to ensure a plate cannot be incorrectly placed for punching? (see illustration)

For Flexo plates, a practice could be used where a visible symbol resembling gear teeth could be imaged on one side of the plate. While that would not physically prevent the wrong orientation, it would make if much more visible than simply imaging the word "gear" in 6-point type on one edge, which is the current practice. Making errors obvious helps to make them more easily spotted when they occur.

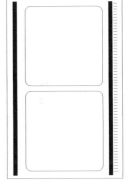

FIGURE 8: *Marking a "gear" visually on the plate can help reduce error by making it easily seen.*

Here is a Poka Yoke example that is a bit more obscure. In commercial print markets, buckle folders are often used for folding signatures for books or sheets for pamphlets or flyers. Each buckle plate must have a calibrated and finely adjusted sheet stop and deflector. One Poka Yoke option to ensure minimal adjustment is to build jigs to momentarily insert into the edges of the buckle plates during initial setup. *(Refer to Figure 5 on page 73)*. The jigs can be premade and coded for common sizes and referenced in the job ticket. Poka Yoke makes sure these codes match during setup, placing the job ticket code in close proximity to the jig code, to ensure a match. This example may or may not directly apply to your plant, but hopefully it gets you thinking about ways you can employ Poka Yoke principles into your setup workflow to ensure correct initial settings. Make the process very difficult to screw up, such that it is very noticeable when an error does occur.

In the previous example, an incorrect initial setup is visible to the operator and anyone walking by. Using the right jig should be obvious. Setting up a system like this helps to make sure that minimal adjustment is needed, the right settings are employed the first time, and that mistakes are not made, which causes wasted time correcting the setup during makeready.

Does this example seem unrealistic to you? Well it may be. But what I hope you walk away with is to get your team thinking about options and discussing them. The goal in your early stages of Setup Reduction is to get the dialog going. To get your operators thinking about Poka Yoke and to let ideas stimulate other ideas. Before you know it, you will have some very workable error-proofing ideas working your company.

An opportunity for Poka Yoke occurs during plate mounting on an offset press to ensure accurate initial registration. A visual mark can be imaged on a plate and used to line up with a comparable mark scribed on the plate clamp. As the plate is mounted, the operator looks at the alignment of the imaged mark and the scribed mark. If they are aligned, the operator has confidence that the plates are mounted in the correct initial position and that initial registration will be accurate. This process may be useful even for pin mounting and automated plate mounting as a means of verification. When a visual cue affirms a mechanical or automated process, it helps to ensure predicable results and identify when systems are out of calibration.

Let us now look at an example of plate mounting for narrow-web flexo on a video mounter. In this situation, how can we Poka Yoke the process to affirm correct initial placement? It may be possible to make a quick verifying instrument so that mounted cylinders are initially cross checked for lateral and tangential registration accuracy (circumferential is infinitely adjustable on most presses and initial macro positioning can be verified when mounting on press). A plexiglass or acrylic sheet with a scale imaged on it can be used to quickly mark register on your key cylinder and then each subsequent cylinder is checked to it. Or, to make it even more reliable, a movable registration pin can be attached to the video mounter to verify lateral position of plates during mounting, should cameras be bumped or moved. Perhaps this is a bit of a stretch but the principle holds true.

Remember, you may not be able to find a Poka Yoke solution today for every mistake scenario. So, the best thing to do is make a large board and label it "Mistakes Needing a Poka Yoke Solution." Anytime an error is discovered, place it on the board. The objective is to develop systems so that mistakes never happen a second time. Experience helps, of course, but Poka Yoke does not rely on experienced operators but rather process standardization so that even inexperienced operators minimize mistakes, or discover them before any ramifications. Raising awareness is the first and most important part of implementing Lean thinking. Sometimes solutions take time. But, simply discounting a problem as being impossible to mistake proof will certainly put it to death. Raise the question, recognize it as a problem, and revisit it often. You may find a solution emerges with time.

Poka Yoke Used to Eliminate Rework

Perhaps an even more costly scenario is when a makeready is performed using the wrong substrate, wrong plates, wrong ink, wrong ink sequence, binding the wrong signature sequence, binding signatures in the wrong orientation, or some other error occurs during makeready. Valuable hours can be wasted reworking a job once the incorrect consumable or parameters are discovered. Here is where a Poka Yoke system can be invaluable during makeready.

During the premakeready phase, systems must be in place to ensure the correct materials have been selected. One strategy is to make sure the job ticket uses cues for picking the correct materials during the premakeready/ staging phase. For example, exact stock samples can be included in the job ticket for visual reference or visual symbols may be used in addition to job numbers, which are much more recognizable for error-detection. All supplies, consumables, and materials are double-checked when pulled and marked or labeled with a "job symbol" as well as a job number.

An alternative is to mark symbols on materials as they arrive as raw materials. Then the symbols are matched with a job. Of course, symbols by themselves are insufficient for verifying the correct material, but in combination with supply names and job numbers, symbols are a nice visual confirmation that the correct materials are being used during makeready. They offer a visual means for operators and those around to ensure accuracy.

During binding, multiple book signatures must be placed in the correct pockets to guarantee the correct page imposition. "Binder's plugs" (collating marks) are used as a visual reference so that signatures are put in the right pocket with the correct orientation. This is an excellent visual solution for the operator and those nearby. One setup is to use a visual reader to immediately flag errors and stop the binder. An even better strategy is to put a reader further upstream in the pocket so that if the wrong signature is even loaded, the stream can be flagged and corrected without stopping the binder. These examples represent two levels of Poka Yoke: a visual method and a technology method.

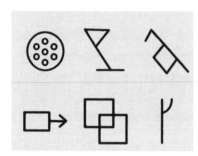

FIGURE 9: *Symbols can be a method to visually match items. It can be easier to distinguish symbols rather than a series of digits.*

I am sure you have seen matching necklaces that, when placed next to each other, form a completed heart. Each individual wears a half heart and when together, the halves match precisely to form a whole. This notion of using two matching symbols forms a powerful visual cue using Poka Yoke to confirm the correct materials. Picture this: when stock is delivered to the press, the symbol on the stock is the matching half of the symbol on the job ticket. When plates are delivered to the press, a symbol on each plate is the matching half to the symbol on the job ticket. When ink is delivered to the press, the symbol on the ink is the matching half to the symbol on the job ticket. When receiving a die, foil, or any other supply, the symbol matches the job ticket symbol.

This is a visual representation of Poka Yoke. It is very easy to mix two pantone numbers up, or to grab 60 lb. stock instead of 70 lb. stock. It happens all the time, because humans make mistakes. But it is highly uncommon to grab a material when the symbols do not interconnect properly, much like a key fits a lock. Even people walking by can see that a symbol on a roll does not match the symbol on a job ticket. But rarely will a six-digit number be cross-referenced by a passerby and noticed as a problem. This is a significant principle. Job codes are ineffective for reducing mistakes. Understanding the power of visual symbols helps to eliminate the problems that occur from humans making mistakes, whether because of fatigue, lack of attention, or simply having a bad day.

We have offered a few examples in this chapter to illustrate the concept of Poka Yoke, and particularly using visual cues for Poka Yoke. The concept of Poka Yoke is simple; make it impossible, or at least very difficult, to do something wrong. Where should you put your focus in your plant? Start with the areas or processes that seem to have the highest occurrence of mistakes or errors. Get your employees involved to identify problem areas or issues and use basic problem solving techniques to list root causes. Then attack each of these with brainstorming sessions on how their occurrence and reoccurrence can be prevented. We have offered a few ideas in this chapter, which may apply to your business:

- Can you use matching symbols to indicate the correct materials?

- Can using matching colors make a process less prone to error?

- What could be added to bring visibility to a problem or defect quicker?

- Would a standardized checklist facilitate a more error-free process?

- What can your employees come up with that prevents mistakes from being repeated?

As with most of Lean concepts, Poka Yoke is not complex. However, it takes employee involvement, management support, resources to experiment with ideas, and recognition and reinforcement when improvements are made. The limits to your improvements rest solely with any limits you put on your organization. Your employees have great knowledge about their jobs and work processes. Use Poka Yoke to guide them along the continuous improvement pathway.

Where do you see Poka Yoke being implemented in your makeready processes?

---

13 When All Else Fails, Reinvent the Process

You have made it to the final step in our Setup Reduction process: when all else fails, reinvent the process. If you have diligently studied and implemented the previous nine steps, I am confident that you have cut your makereadies by 40-50%, and likely more. We see that fairly regularly from those who are serious about Setup Reduction. Of course, you must institutionalize your new practices if you want to maintain those gains. A question does arise about now: How do I get even better improvements? After all, when you really get excited about Setup Reduction, you cannot be satisfied with a 20 or 30-minute makeready.

In order to cut your makeready time and cost further, you may want to consider two options. First, you should revisit all steps again, in sequence. You should video your makeready, and then break it down by internal and external processes again. You should reassess your fasteners and tools. You should look at putting your tools and supplies at the point of use. You should look at your initial settings and strive for "single-move" adjustments. And be sure to standardize and rehearse your setup again. Go through all those steps again and see where additional efficiencies can be gained.

However, when all else fails, reinvent the process.

If you want to get further gains, you will need to figure out new ways to reduce makeready time. We often talk about the standard for setup time as 0 minutes; not 20 minutes, not 10 minute, but zero minutes. Most conventional printers look at us like we are crazy. I can understand why they think that but consider why that becomes our goal.

First, if I tell you that you need to cut your makeready by 10%, you will work faster. If I tell you that you need to cut your makeready by 90%, you will work differently. You have no choice. You cannot cut that much time by doing the same things faster. You will need to do things differently—even reinvent how we think of setup.

Now consider another perspective. If I tell you I have a press that can run with zero setup, what would you say? If you are a conventional printer, you will say, "Show me." If you are a digital printer, you will say, "So, me too." The point is that your perspective or paradigm is everything. Digital presses largely are zero-makeready presses. Of course, they mostly run standardized substrates of standard size and standard color toners or ink. So that may differ from your environment a lot but it is important not to get too enamored with your existing perspective of what a makeready is. Manufacturers are doing a lot to improve makeready times on presses and finishing equipment. Having an open mind to the notion of zero-makeready processes is not only important, it is vital to achieve where you want to go with your business.

Think Big

So, if you want to be serious about being a Lean printer and having enviable setup times—world-class makereadies—then you definitely need to think big and way outside the box. You need to get your process experts to really question everything and be creative. You need to build a culture of inquiry and avoid the temptation of saying, "That is just the way it is. We can't lower makeready time any more than that." It is so easy to fall into that trap.

Among the ways to do that is to look to other companies, especially those outside the printing industry. There are number of manufacturers who have remarkably similar issues to us in the printing field. They deal with customized work, using highly variable processes with a fairly traditional workforce. It is helpful to identify those companies in your community who struggle with similar issues and begin to network.

You will also want to work with suppliers who have similar values. You will want to because these are the companies who are providing you value. These suppliers can produce just in time product because they have reduced their setup times. And they are focused on bringing you value, as their customer.

Many suppliers are a great resource for you. Several paper companies, both mills and merchants, are actively engaging in consulting with their customers to help improve their workflow and reduce equipment setup time. Take advantage of these companies. Press and finishing equipment manufacturers are also active in this arena, hoping to provide a value-added service.

But above all, think big. Face your challenges by documenting the wasteful aspects of your makereadies, even if you have no solutions for your problems. Those who lead in Setup Reduction are those who have no fear of calling waste what it is: waste.

Looking to Technology

We have always suggested that the fastest and cheapest way to saving money through Setup Reduction is to work on the people part and save the new technology improvements for later. We stand by that strategy. Technology can offer substantial benefits, but certainly at a cost. Your human resources can also offer substantial benefits, and often at a lower investment. But perhaps more important than the investment is the competitive advantage you will gain. Your equipment mix can easily be replicated, unless of course you invent/engineer your own equipment. But your culture and your methods cannot easily be replicated. Your biggest competitive advantage is with your people not your equipment.

Having said that, it does make sense to look to technology when you have successful reduced your setup time to a minimum. So, what technologies should you look at? Clearly this book is not the appropriate medium for specifics, but let me touch on a few items.

JDF and CIP4

First, computer integrated manufacturing (CIM), and CIP4/JDF make a great deal of sense in the context of this book. Anytime you can have equipment help you with precise presets, it directly achieves the goals we have written about by reducing needed adjustments. Modern presses and binders are capable of setting up many standard settings for infeed/feeder, delivery, printing units, ink and water balance, pre-inking, automated plate mounting, and so on. For binders, pockets, stitching heads, knives, and most other components can be preset. Modern equipment certainly requires substantial integration and IT infrastructures but if you produce a reasonable volume of work, the savings accrued in your setups may well justify the expense. To stay competitive with other printers, a certain level of investment certainly is necessary and a large investment may supplement the work you have done on the people side of your Setup Reduction.

Servo Technologies

The second technology to consider is the use of servo-mechanical equipment. Besides their ability to control tensions and interactions between printing units or binding components, one of their attractive features is the ability to decouple components, facilitating better parallel processing. If you can advance a printing unit independent of other units, it certainly makes parallel processing more convenient and safer. Servo technology replaces a central drive shaft, thus using many smaller motors for driving the equipment components. Usually servo equipment is more expensive that conventional equipment and is more sophisticated electrically.

Evaluate Equipment with Setup Reduction in Mind

Before concluding this chapter, I would like to emphasize that the equipment-purchasing matrix you use for evaluating equipment should be revisited with Setup Reduction in mind. After you have spent substantial time working with Setup Reduction, you will have a good sense of where your challenges remain. Before you purchase any new equipment, make sure you video and analyze your makeready on your existing equipment, with all improved processes utilized. This practice will give you a good understanding where you still need to improve.

For example, let suppose you start this process with 60-minute makereadies. After working through the initial nine steps, you get your average makeready time down to 35 minutes. Congratulations, by the way. But now you have decided to purchase a new CIP4 compatible press so that you can take advantage of the new technologies that are out there. Before you do that, you spend some time analyzing your 35-minute makeready and realize that some of that time is a result of poor staging. Operators still have to track down supplies. How will this new CIP4 piece of equipment improve your makeready time? You may find that you are still doing 35-minute setups. How disappointing will that be?

Or, you may look at that video and find out that you are spending 15-minutes putting plates on the press because they must be done one at a time and your procedures seems particularly slow. You may find out that changing your procedure would help some but that you really need to invest in automatic plate changing technology, which you had not considered a priority before. Like all purchasing decisions, you need to make informed selections. It is easy to be enamored by technology but what you really need are practical solutions for how you do a makeready. You have invested many hours and days working on Setup Reduction. Make sure your technology supports that effort, not the other way around.

Invent Your Own Equipment

To conclude this chapter, I want to discuss the notion of you inventing your own technology. That is a daunting thought for most small and medium-sized printers. I understand that. But you may find that you can work with a local machinist or engineer to develop some small retrofit on your existing press or binder. You should also discuss your ideas with your preferred equipment manufacturers. They may be willing to let you beta test some designs, which of course they will incorporate on new equipment offerings in the future.

For the larger companies with internal engineering departments, by all means, take advantage of that group to help you develop Poka Yoke solutions, as well as methods for improving adjustments. Use your teams to make common fasteners or invent some quick-release screw systems.

The best printers in the world are those who devote time, energy, and resources to create a competitive advantage by creating new processes. If you want to be a world-class printer, you too can develop new ways to speed makeready and reduce the wasted time of adjusting registration and setting color.

Where have you exhausted all Setup Reduction gains and need to reinvent your makeready process?

14 Taking the Next Step

At this point, you have received a lot of information about Setup Reduction for the printing industry. An obvious question at this point is what do you do with all this information and how do you get started with your own Setup Reduction process in your facility? This chapter will help you get focused on the key elements to maximize your ability to achieve Setup Reductions in your operation.

Educating Everyone

The key to getting started is—getting started. There is no magical recipe or formula to understand to begin your Lean journey and implement Setup Reduction principles. Lean is an iterative process where individual and organizational learning and understanding grow over time. Can you benchmark what others have done? Sure. Can you hold meetings and outline a grand strategy or master plan to follow? Sure. Will doing either of these steps help? Sure, but they are *not* essential.

What is essential is choosing to go down the Lean pathway and get your own people educated and involved in the process. Your journey will be unique to your situation. Your pace will match your needs and your desire to change and evolve into a Lean printer. Your progress will be impeded only by your energy and your commitment to embracing the concepts outlined in the previous chapters. Commitment to Lean is not lip service; it is managing by clearly and consistently backing a relentless movement towards making the business more Lean.

Education of your employees is a key driver to move Lean forward in your facility. Lean is seen by many as a common sense alternative to the normal ways businesses have evolved into with convoluted processes, waste built into the "way we do things here", and an inherent resistance to changing things for the better. As employees learn about Lean in general, and Setup Reduction in particular, they quickly grasp the concepts and become enthused about embracing the principles in their unique workspace and equipment areas. This happens because employees recognize the value associated with Lean principles and how Lean will make their jobs easier, create more value for their customers, and make their jobs more secure, as their company will benefit as well.

Like every Lean concept or tool, Setup Reduction is dependent on solid 5s principles being in place for benefits to be realized and for the tool to work well. A work area cannot be improved, nor have the improvements that are made sustained, without 5s fundamentals already established. 5s, like educating and empowering your employees, is fundamental to your Lean journey. Organizations need to invest in the Lean fundamentals of 5s, team building, and empowerment to capitalize on the tools of Lean, Setup Reduction included.

Communication, Consistency of Purpose, Clarity of Direction

To implement Setup Reduction, management needs to get in front of the process and lead through example. Foundational to Lean success is the use of empowered work teams to allow employees the opportunity to engage in the principles and impact their job processes in a positive manner. Empowerment does not mean abdication or loss of control by managers. On the contrary, control is still required by managers in setting targets, goals, and determining acceptable behaviors within the organization. Ideally, this is done through the use of mission and vision statements that help state the values and direction of your business. A well-defined, and well-used, mission statement can prove invaluable to help employees determine appropriate behaviors and to guide their actions in times of decision.

Becoming Lean requires a lot from managers in the way of communication. Embarking on a Lean journey will take your business into new places and into different ways of defining value than you have used in the past. Change creates uncertainty, which can cause employees to become more timid about making decisions and enacting change; both of which will delay your Lean progress. Management must understand they cannot over communicate about the Lean journey they have embarked upon.

Think about how you communicate with a grown, mature adult about something simple such as printing a book. If the adult is familiar at all with books or printing you can make some broad generalizations and quickly gauge whether you are effectively making the points you want to with them. Now take the same conversation but have it with a young child. Not only can you not make many assumptions about what they already know about books or printing, but most statements you make have to come with a contextual reference the child can relate to if you really want them to understand anything about printing a book. You can take this example and apply it to how you need to communicate about becoming Lean in your organization. While I am not trying to imply your employees are, or act, like young children, your organizational maturity on the topic of Lean and empowerment is likely on the less mature end of the spectrum compared to companies who have been undertaking a Lean initiative for many years. This is the context managers have to keep in mind as they communicate about Lean. Your employees will embrace the Lean concepts readily. Your goal is to find the means to enable employees to take action steps and not be encumbered by any confusion about the goals of Lean or what management wants to accomplish with Lean initiatives.

So what are some good ways to educate everyone? You certainly have one in your hands now, a book describing Lean and the tools of Lean can go a long ways. In the back of this book we have a list of some of our favorite Lean books; you can use these or certainly find your own that relate best to your thinking and way of doing things. If your employees do not have time to read, think about having employees teach each other Lean concepts by giving out each chapter of a book to different employees. Let the individual employee just read and become expert on a single chapter; then be prepared to explain and relate that chapter to other employees in how the ideas apply to your business. An idea would be to designate an hour and a chapter a week; in fifteen weeks you have covered fully a fifteen-chapter book and no one had to read or specialize in more than a single chapter! As the topics unfold, you may well find the interest increases and employees start reading things they are not assigned and pushing you, and the organization, to go faster to become educated on Lean.

Seminars are a terrific way to get a few employees educated and excited about the potential of Lean in your business. Again, in the back of this book we provide some examples of Lean seminars that provide a good overview for employees. It is rare to have someone attend a good Lean seminar and not get fired up about what becoming Lean could do for their job and your business. This can be a cost-effective means of getting some Lean momentum going in your plant. Sometimes, if you sense certain employees are going to be resistant to the principles of Lean (or change in general) then sending those people specifically to a seminar where they can ask their questions away from the work environment and while they are in the company of others who are thinking about becoming Lean can prove valuable in winning them over to Lean thinking.

Some firms bring in consultants to help educate and jumpstart the Lean process. We believe in this, but only to a point. Consultants can do a wonderful job in conveying information, educating employees and management, spotting waste and helping to point firms in the right direction, but ultimately your company and your management has to own the Lean change process. You cannot outsource your Lean transformation or write checks to someone to make you Lean. Your company will become Lean through your involvement, engagement, and understanding of the Lean process and this cannot be purchased or delivered to you anyway other than through your own efforts.

So again, how do you best start becoming Lean? You start! You educate! You communicate! You lead! You support your employees' efforts as they begin to understand Lean. You recognize you do not have every answer or an outline of every step you will, or should, take but you are committed to moving relentlessly forward with Lean concepts firmly in mind and an emphasis on continually educating yourself and your employees on what it means to become Lean to help guide you down the road.

What steps will you make to initiate Setup Reduction?

_____

_____

_____

_____

_____

_____

_____

_____

_____

15 Achieving Lasting Improvement

In the beginning of this book we spoke of "Being Lean" versus "Doing Lean," another way to look at this is through the comparison of enacting cultural change or simply implementing a tool. To better explain the thought here we will try to make a few comparisons to illustrate the point.

You can teach someone the fundamental principles around using all of a mechanic's tools but it does not make them a mechanic (or at least not a good one). Good mechanics know how to trouble-shoot, how to problem solve, how to prevent future issues from arising, and how to analyze complex situations to determine root causes of issues and how best to resolve them. Knowing how their tools work provides a rudimentary education but does not offer the richness or depth required to be good at the mechanic craft.

Similarly, you could show me how to set color on a four-color press and I could fully understand what button moves which ink key and which direction to push it to get more or less ink onto the substrate. Additionally, I could understand ink and water balance perfectly in principle but full knowledge of all of this would not make me good at quickly setting color correctly to match a customer's expectation with minimal waste. In addition to the knowledge of what to do in concept, it takes experience, problem solving ability, multi-tasking skills, crew leadership, trouble-shooting, and a myriad of other skills to do this well. It is not enough to know how to do it in principle; it takes experience and practice to do it professionally and well.

Another example that is hitting close to home at our house is a teenager learning to drive. Through the permit process and driver education, along with years of observing parents drive them around town and on trips, teens have a pretty thorough understanding of how to accelerate, steer, brake, and turn a car. Knowing how it all works to go forward, backwards, faster, park, and stop is very different than being a proficient and safe driver. There are many things involved in driving that simply cannot be learned until you experience them yourself. Think of the first time you drove in the snow, or hit ice, or found yourself in a dense fog bank, or the person next to you suddenly swerved into your space. We can talk about these events, perhaps in a simulator you can attempt to experience them, but as we are all aware it is very different to experience the variety of challenges that get thrown your way when you are actually driving a vehicle and only time behind the wheel helps to prepare you for them.

So, the point from these examples is this: Setup Reduction concepts are simple in principle. There is probably nothing in the text of this book that stumped you or seemed impossible to do. However, there is a vast difference between simply trying to implement the concepts of Setup Reduction on top of how you already do business (what we would term "Doing Lean" and would strongly advise against) versus actually "Being Lean" and fundamentally rethinking the way you manage your business under the concepts of Lean thinking.

Being Lean means enacting cultural change to fully embrace Lean think-ing. Being Lean means empowering your employees, fostering teamwork, rewarding teamwork and improvement initiatives that reinforce Lean thinking, and committing and communicating exhaustively about your Lean journey. It includes having the fortitude and commitment to fund Lean with resources to nurture it through good times and bad because you fundamentally believe it is the right direction to take your business.

Sustaining Improvement Efforts

Most people resist change and will actively work to keep things the way they are. Change is perceived as a threat to be avoided or attacked. Frequently this is done in very subtle ways at all levels in the organization. This point applies just as much to company management as it does to employees. To some extent, everyone has a vested interest in keeping things the way they currently are; it is just easier to do. This is one of the primary reasons companies tend to take the easy, but incorrect, way out in implementing Lean and just try to insert Lean tools on top of how they currently do things.

The practice of 5s is fundamental to any Lean implementation. Truthfully, 5s is hard. On the other hand, 4S is easy. That troublesome 5th S, sustain, is where it gets difficult and where the companies who truly understand Lean separate themselves from those who are looking for quick fixes and will move on to the next flavor-of-the-month improvement plan quickly.

Management needs to ask how they can actively and publically make change acceptable, wanted and rewarded. The status quo cannot be accepted or used to justify not making improvement steps within the business. Lean is totally about managing the entire business, not just improving manufacturing processes. If a company wants to sustain their improvement gains they will learn how to build a culture that expects, and demands, change initiatives from employees and from management.

Principles are like values, they should be applied consistently not just when it is convenient. To sustain Lean in your organization, the principles surrounding Lean must be embraced and practiced always; not just when times are good or when it seems like an easy time to get something done with the Lean effort.

The process does matter. It is not just about getting results (however you did it). Printers are notorious for "doing whatever it takes" to get a job out the door or to satisfy a customer desire. This has long been viewed as an admirable trait and, in fact, employees have been noted in their performance appraisals in a positive manner for displaying this attribute. The problem with this approach is it fundamentally fails to address root-causes of problems or effectively deal with issues to prevent their reoccurrence. People get so focused on getting a job out the door that existing processes get bypassed, rules are broken, procedures are not followed, and employees get the clear message that nothing is sacred and rules and principles mean nothing. Do not kid yourself; that is the message you send when the focus shifts to results regardless of the process to achieve them. Those printers who wish to be Lean will recognize this behavior as detrimental to their efforts and will understand the need to rethink how they do business.

Process change means *change*, not layering new things on top of old ways of doing business. Setup Reduction means change. Firms that embrace Lean recognize that all their assumptions about how they do business are fair game for questioning, altering, and improving. Management can aid this in Lean by striving to make things visible. Lean is a very visual concept. Visibility is used to show performance, facilitate standard work, aid employees in their jobs, and to show where processes are not performing as expected. When in doubt, find a way to bring visibility to a process as a means of improving it. When problems arise, or continue, in a given process, find the means to break it down into further, or simpler steps and bring visibility to these to aid improvement. Lean practitioners make it a point to make problems visible so as to bring needed resources to fix them. Conventional thinking encourages people to hide problems and move on in an effort to get work out; this is the antithesis of Lean thinking and will derail your efforts to sustain Lean gains.

Management is key to sustaining Lean in a company. Managers need to be visible by having an ongoing presence on the factory floor. Lean believers solve problems by going to the source of issues, not by reading reports in a distant office or trying to decipher events from metrics produced after the event occurred. *Management by walking around* is an old principle but one that applies well to Lean. Empowering a workforce does not mean you abandon it; rather, empowerment requires greater management involvement than conventional management theory, where control is exercised through rules and the power of discipline for not adhering to established rules. Having a management presence on the floor to see what is actually taking place is essential for sustaining Lean. When managers see what is actually going on they are better equipped to provide the needed resources to fully problem solve and eliminate issues permanently.

Many companies use the Lean tool of Kaizen to aid their change process in becoming Lean. Kaizen means to improve for the better and supports the continuous improvement principle of Lean management. Teaching employees the Kaizen process, and allowing them to use it as an ongoing tool to improve work processes, will also help you sustain your Lean efforts. Kaizen should not be used as a "once in a while" event driven tool; rather Kaizen should become part of your Lean arsenal that is commonly and frequently used to improve your business.

Creating a Durable Competitive Advantage

The goal of every business is to create a durable competitive advantage. You want to excel, you want to be better than the competition, you want to be preferred by your customers, and you want to command a pricing premium or be significantly lower in your costs. Educating your company, understanding, and implementing Setup Reduction is a means to achieving these goals. Conventional understanding has taught generations that business is a zero-sum endeavor. To get something you have to give something else up. Resources are limited and choices have to be made. Traditional thinking insists that trade-offs exist for every decision; Lean thinkers do not believe or accept this as a constraint on the organization. Lean is not a manufacturing value; it is a strategic value. Accepting Lean is a decision about altering the way you view your business and the choices you make. It is a way to change the way your organization approaches the customer/supplier relationship.

Setup Reduction is an excellent way to build customer value. Quick gains can be made with just a little effort. But the deep and significant gains will come only with relentless focus and concentrated efforts. It will not come through a single champion. It will happen as a result of trained, motivated and empowered employees. It is through your engaged team, powered by your strong vision, and immersed in a broader Lean culture that Setup Reduction will impact your business in a sustainable way. And when it does, you will be unbeatable in the marketplace! Setup Reduction and Lean are a lifestyle, not an event. We wish you much success in your own Setup Reduction journey.

What changes are needed for your organization to develop a durable competitive advantage?

_____

_____

_____

_____

_____

_____

_____

_____

Appendix A

List of Lean Resources to Consider in Your Lean Journey

Cooper, Kevin, Keif, Malcolm G., and Macro, Kenneth L. (2007). *Lean Printing: Pathway to Success.* Pittsburgh: PIA/GATF Press

Cooper, Kevin (2010). *Lean Printing: Cultural Imperatives for Success.* Pittsburgh: PIA/GATF Press

Rizzo, Ken (2001). *Total Production Maintenance.* Pittsburgh: PIA/GATF Press

Mann, David (2005). *Creating a Lean Culture.* New York: Productivity Press

Kotter, John (1996). *Leading Change.* Boston: Harvard Business School Press

Henderson, Bruce A., and Larco, Jorge L. (2002). *Lean Transformation.* Richmond: The Oaklea Press

Martin, Stephen Hawley (2005). *Lean Enterprise Leader.* Richmond: The Oklea Press

Liker, Jeffrey K. (2004). *The Toyota Way.* New York: McGraw-Hill

Liker, Jeffrey K., and Meier, David (2006). *The Toyota Way Fieldbook.* New York: McGraw-Hill

Emiliani, Bob (2007 – 2010). *Real Lean – Volumes One through Six.* Kensington: The Center for Lean Business Management, LLC

Galsworth, Gwendolyn D. (2005). *Visual Workplace.* Portland: Visual-Lean® Enterprise Press

Galsworth, Gwendoly D. (2011). *Work That Makes Sense.* Portland: Visual-Lean® Enterprise Press

Appendix B

Lean Resources and Seminars

At Cal Poly, San Luis Obispo we present Lean workshops geared to serve the graphic communication industry. You can find information on upcoming events at this link: *http://grci.calpoly.edu/index.html*

Professors Keif and Cooper have run workshops for companies across the United States, Canada, Europe, and the Middle East. They are available for consultation and can be contacted directly at: *mkeif@calpoly.edu* and *klcooper@calpoly.edu*

The Printing Industries of America offers a Lean selection of books and webinars for your continuing education. Their selection can be found at: *http://www.printing.org/store/142*

While not directly related to the graphic communication industry, Performance, Instruction, and Training offers PIT crew training which focuses on Lean principles in reducing change-over and setup times. Information can be found at: *http://www.visitpit.com/group-lean-training/half-day-training/*

The Continuous Improvement Conference is an annual PIA event bringing together printers who are engaged in, or interested in learning about, Lean initiatives. Information at: *http://ci.printing.org*